The Small Business Owner's Guide To Local Lead Generation

Proven Strategies & Tips To Grow Your Business!

Ray L. Perry, Justin Sturges, Phil Singleton, Kevin Jordan, Mark Z. Fortune

The Small Business Owner's Guide To Local Lead Generation

What Others Are Saying about *The Small Business Owner's Guide to Local Lead Generation*

"The Small Business Owner's Guide to Local Lead Generation *is your ticket to success. Get it right now!*"

John Jantsch
Bestselling author of *Duct Tape Marketing*

"This book contains the real, hands-on stuff that you need to understand, do and master in order to survive and thrive online today."

Michael Port
New York Times bestselling author of *Book Yourself Solid*

"As a small business owner, you don't have a war chest of money to burn on marketing and advertising. What you need is a way to take smarter action that gets the right results. Read this book and you'll see more leads come in, period."

Brian Clark
CEO, Copyblogger Media

"This is a great resource for any local business that is trying to figure out how they can generate leads and ultimately revenue for their business. I highly recommend it."

Dan Olson
CEO, UpCity.com

"While skeptical when I was first approached to review this book, I was pleasantly surprised by the insight and value the The Small Business Owner's Guide To Local Lead Generation *book provides. I feel though that the value they are offering extends well beyond just local lead generation and can easily apply to David and Goliath situations in non-local businesses. What I like the most is its emphasis on understanding your users, and the need to apply sweat equity into the process, not chase the latest tactics and trends. I will be sharing this book with my own marketing team, and recommend you do as well. Wading through the mountain of noise on the web is difficult, when you come across practical sound advice, you have to jump on it!"*

Tony Perez
Co-Founder / CEO at Sucuri, Inc.

"Smart small business owners realize that they have significant advantages over their larger, more cumbersome competition. This book will teach you how to fight with the big guys and win."

Eric Enge
CEO of Stone Temple Consulting
Author of *The Art Of SEO*

"Growing your small business is hard, and you need to find customers to do it. The Small Business Owner's Guide to Local Lead Generation will help you make it happen."

Mike McDerment
Co-founder and CEO, FreshBooks

"Since I work with a lot of small businesses, I see first hand how big of an impact local search and marketing has. I'd recommend The Small Business Owners Guide to Local Lead Generation to any small business owner who wants to start developing and implementing the same strategies big companies do to dominate their local market."

Kelsey Jones
Executive Editor at Search Engine Journal

"This is a great book for small business owners looking to connect with local prospects and customers without spending a lot of time or money. It's written by marketing experts with simple ideas and case studies that will help them grow their businesses!"

Jon Ferrara
CEO, Nimble

"Our small business clients are always looking to grow through smart, effective approaches to marketing. The Small Business Owner's Guide to Local Lead Generation *is the guide our clients need to really help drive their businesses forward."*

J. Phillip Jett
President Central Arkansas, IBERIABANK

"The Duct Tape Marketing Consultants spell out practical, affordable steps for small business owners to map out strategies to make the phone ring. This book is what the business owner needs - a quick read, but the keys to blending traditional and digital marketing for successful brand awareness and lead generation."

Tracey Osborne
President, Overland Park Chamber of Commerce

"Are you a small business David surveying a field crowded with big business Goliaths? This book gives you the smooth stones for your marketing sling to bring those Goliaths down. You don't need to be bigger or richer than those Goliaths, you just need the wisdom in this book!"

Mark Traphagen,
Senior Director of Online Marketing,
Stone Temple Consulting

"There are a plethora of books available to help business owners looking to generate new business, but this concise book is powerfully packed with easy to implement, practical and money generating ideas. It is specifically geared to take the small business owner to the next level. If you are looking for concrete ideas to boost your bottom line The Small Business Owner's Guide to Local Lead Generation *is the book for you."*

Dawne Brooks Gulla
Executive Director, BNI Central Virginia

"This guide empowers small business owners to take control of their marketing and bring more customers in the door. These are not one-time hacks but easy to understand lessons that are both cost-effective and repeatable. Competitors will be left scratching their heads."

Mickie Kennedy
President of eReleases

"One of the biggest problems that small businesses face is how to generate leads and revenue. The authors of this book not only recognize how important it is for businesses today to come up with a cost effective marketing strategy, but they also outline every step of the process. Whether you're just getting started as a small local business or want to improve your existing marketing strategy, read this book. Your clients will thank you."

Philip Petrescu
Founder and CEO of Advanced Web Ranking

"All revenue starts with a good lead source. This book breaks down the process of generating leads and turning them into revenue. And most important, for small business owners without dedicated marketing staff and living with tight budgets, the information is to the point, practical, and designed to provide a competitive edge."

Kelly Scanlon
President & CEO, Thinking Bigger Business Media, Inc.

"I talk to small business owners all the time who struggle with bringing in new customers. It turns out it's because they haven't read this book yet! These guys are true marketing pros who start with the strategy and then deliver on great tactics that work in today's challenging environment. It's simple - read this, implement and get more business."

Shawn Kinkade

President, Aspire Business Development, Board Director
Leawood Chamber of Commerce

"The Small Business Owner's Guide to Local Lead Generation *perfectly addresses the struggles of businesses trying to build online presence and provides actionable advice. It's a must-read for any small business owner."*

Ann Smarty

Brand Manager at Internet Marketing Ninjas

Foreword

Can the Little Guy Actually Win?

Every company needs to be strategic in its marketing, no matter whether it's a big multinational corporation or a small local business. The five authors of this book, as Duct Tape Marketing Consultants, have "strategy before tactics" as a core principle of their businesses. So it's no surprise that their approach to helping local businesses to thrive involves a focus first on strategy before delving into some powerful marketing tactics. But the results they've been able to deliver for their clients speak volumes about the soundness of this principle!

Even in the shadow of large companies with multi-million dollar marketing budgets, these guys have cracked the code for helping generate high-quality leads for small, local businesses. Each of the authors has used what they've learned through their extensive training and experience to help local business owners successfully implement the tactics described in this book. After getting to know each other as members of the Duct Tape Marketing Consultant Network, they decided to collaborate on a definitive guide for small business owners looking to compete more effectively.

This team of small business marketing consultants, web designers & Internet marketers has worked with thousands of small businesses owners just like you. Mark, Kevin, Ray, Phil and Justin have been hired over and over again for the sole purpose of helping small businesses get to the next level. They know what tactics stand the test of time, and what emerging web strategies and tactics are producing the best results today. This book takes the guesswork out of local lead generation. Period.

I think they've done a terrific job in outlining the strategic advantage a locally-owned business has over the big guys — and then giving a practical explanation of the most effective tactics for generating leads, both online and off-line. Right in line with the core of the Duct Tape Marketing brand, this book offers expert and actionable advice that can enable a small business to outsmart and outmaneuver businesses a hundred times their size.

As you read through this book, you'll note that the authors take a decidedly web-centric approach to marketing. There is no doubt that traditional forms of marketing such as event and referral marketing are more important than ever. Yet, in today's world, all roads lead back to your company's website. People may have heard about your company at a seminar, on the radio or through a friend, but your ideal customers are more than likely going to look you up online at some point along the purchase path. You see, your website in no longer just a "site on the web", it's the hub of all of your marketing efforts. By the end of this book, you will stop thinking about your website as the stepchild of your business, and start weaving it into the fold of your daily routine. Once you have the right marketing plan and the right digital platform in place, all you need to do is apply the right combination of tactics consistently. This book shows you how to do it.

Also as you read on, please take into consideration that the way this book was created, how it was marketed and promoted and how the book's website and social media channels are being used to amplify the messaging – all perfect examples of how you should be marketing your own business. A central theme to Duct Tape Marketing is creating great content for your ideal customers. That includes blog posts, videos, podcasts, press releases, eBooks, white papers and yes, sometimes even publishing a real book. As I mentioned above, many of the strategies detailed herein are web-centric. As you read more, you will find that the book comes with a companion website (www.LocalLeadGenBook.com) with as much (if not more) great content in the form of tips, examples, blog posts, videos, newsletters and other resources – including a free eBook: 66 Local Lead Gen Tactics. In other words, the authors are practicing what they preach by creating great content and driving their ideal customers to their website, where you can continue the ongoing education process and adding value to your business long after you have read this book and referred it or passed it along to a friend. You will get as much value from reading the book as you will studying the website, the digital ecosystem that was constructed around it, and the way the book was launched.

If you own a small, local business – or are responsible for marketing one – you need to read this book now, and then take action on what you read. The Small Business Owner's Guide To Local Lead Generation is the real deal. And don't just take my word for it – be sure to read though the endorsements. This book has been recommended by an impressive list of marketing and business thought leaders, technology company executives and other best-selling authors. If you implement the advice you're about to read, this might just be the year you take a bite out of the market share your competitors thought they had in the bag.

John Jantsch
Author, *Duct Tape Marketing, Duct Tape Selling*
and *The Referral Engine*

Table of Contents

Chapter One: It's Not Easy Being the Little Guy

"Small business isn't for the faint of heart. It's for the brave, the patient and the persistent. It's for the overcomer."

Unknown

You didn't choose the easiest path in life, you know. You could have chosen a job where you punched a clock and picked up a check every couple of weeks. You could have pursued a career that you'd leave at the office every night when you went home – and didn't even think about on weekends.

But no, not you.

You chose small business ownership. You eat what you go out and hunt and kill and drag home. You built your business from nothing – or took it over (which might even be harder).

You've heard the joke before, right?

Owning a business is great because you only have to work half-days.
… You choose which 12 hours you work each day.

Even though your days (and nights and weekends, by and large) are filled with a lot of hard work, more than your share of tension headaches, the occasional moment of all-out panic, and an odd assortment of situations and challenges you never dreamed you'd face, there's also a sense of satisfaction you get from having your own business that nobody in a 'normal' job gets to enjoy. You've built your business with your own hands, mind, and nerves of steel.

You know what it is to learn on the fly. You're no stranger to working odd hours (and lots of them) to make sure you get it all done. You've tweaked your internal systems and processes to make your business run as smoothly as possible (a wise survival tactic!). You've handled everything from stocking inventory and supplies to collections, from hiring and firing to plunging the toilet, from filing and bookkeeping to fielding phone calls.

You've done it all – and not necessarily because it was fun. You do what you have to in order to keep the doors open and serve your customers. That's what we do as small business owners – whatever it takes.

Some days and years are more challenging than others. If you've seen big competitors creeping into your local market, you've experienced some challenges that left you wondering how you'd survive.

Competing against big businesses can seem like an exercise in futility. They seem to have it all – more money to pay for advertising, staffing, equipment, and inventory. You name it, it seems like they've got it. They can throw money at problems and opportunities in ways you just can't.

Seems like the advantage clearly goes to the big guy. Slam dunk.

But wait.

That's not actually the case.

What if we told you that you could not only stay afloat in your local market, but that you could actually dominate your bigger competitors? What if we said that it didn't matter that your competitors have seemingly bottomless buckets of money to use in marketing? And what if you discovered that it's actually YOU who holds a significant market advantage when it comes to attracting and engaging new local customers for your business… and that your bigger competitors had better watch out because you're about to eat their lunch?

It's true.

You have some advantages the big guys can't match. You've just got to know how to use them. The truth is, the people you really want to have as your customers would overwhelmingly prefer to do business with you instead of going to the huge, impersonal company down the road from you. The trick is in being strategic so that you can identify, then go after your ideal customers.

That's where this book comes in.

You see, the five of us specialize in helping businesses just like yours. We're all Certified Duct Tape Marketing Consultants, which means we've got extensive training and experience working with small business owners to help them identify, attract, and convert more ideal customers, so that their business doesn't just survive… it grows just as big as they want it to be.

You're about to find out exactly what you need to do for your business so that it becomes much more simple to claim the market share you want, no matter who else moves into your territory. This is the book your big competitors hope you won't read, because they know if you do, they'll lose their size advantage and soon find themselves watching all the good customers head your way.

Oh, and don't worry. We know that sneaking away to read for a few minutes is nearly impossible – and the last thing you can afford is to be lulled to sleep for an unexpected (but probably desperately needed) nap. So we get right to the point, and do it in a way that you'll enjoy reading.

Are you ready?

Chapter Two: Can't Out-Spend Them? Better Out-Think Them

"When an underdog fought like David, he usually won. But most underdogs don't fight like David."

Malcolm Gladwell

David and Goliath

So you're a small fish in a big pond. You've had near-miss scuffles with sharks and other fish big enough to steal your lunch and eat it right in front of you and then polish you off as dessert. Even if you own a business that's been around for generations, you might feel a tad intimidated by the sheer size of your competitors – and rightfully so, because many local businesses simply can't throw cash at problems the way large corporations can. Every move you make counts.

You might feel like you're facing an eventually fatal disadvantage – but that's not necessarily true. If you use the resources and advantages you've got as a small business, you can out-perform even the biggest competitors in your area.

As a local business, you've got some advantages over your bigger competitors. You're probably more nimble than the big guys – an advantage that's nothing to sneeze at, enabling you to implement while your bigger competitors' latest and greatest strategy is still stuck in committee. You've also got the great equalizer working in your favor; small businesses can use technology just as effectively as big ones can.

But the biggest advantage you've got in your corner is that starting right now, you can out-strategize local competitors of any size and win. With smarter strategies as the base of your growth campaign, every dollar and every minute you spend on tactics will hit its mark. By putting strategy first, you'll avoid the otherwise irresistible quest for shiny objects that derails other business owners, big and small. While they're chasing their tails, barking up all the wrong trees, and investing heavily in tactics that nobody can even measure the effectiveness of, you'll be making steady progress toward your growth goals.

Forget Ready, Fire, Aim – Just for a Moment

That's a great way to express the benefits of taking action before waiting for complete certainty and clarity – but it doesn't work so well without a sound strategy in place first. All the tactics, tools, and tricks in the world won't make up for not having your strategy nailed down first.

The cornerstone of your business growth strategy is so simple that many businesses overlook it completely. It is two-pronged, and addresses what you sell, and who you want to sell it to.

First, what do you REALLY sell?

Now you might think you sell car insurance, dental care, electrical services, or whatever is printed on your business license. But you don't. Not really.

What you sell is your power to make problems disappear. Could be a problem related to a vehicle, a tooth, or an outlet – but whatever it is, it's bothersome enough for your customers to seek your help. Whether your products and services represent solutions for the necessities of daily life or optional luxuries, you're selling a better life to your customers.

Your customers and prospects have more choices available than ever before. Even in small towns, there's usually more than one butcher, one baker, and one candlestick maker. That means your customers have to choose the one they think will be best for them. One will stick out from the crowd and appear to them as the best choice – the one that's the perfect fit, the one that'll take the best care of them, the one that'll understand their problem and make it go away.

What's odd is that you may not even know what you sell. Your customers can tell you – if you ask them. They'll tell you exactly why they prefer doing business with you instead of your competitors. They'll even tell you what drew them to you in the first place, what keeps them coming back, and what makes them eager to tell their friends and neighbors about you.

They won't just come out with it; you'll need to ask. It will probably feel strange, and maybe even a bit vulnerable to ask, "Why do you do business with me?" Part of your mind might start squawking, saying you should be worried that by prompting them to think about it, they'll re-evaluate their buying decision and go with your competitor. No doubt you'll think you already know the answer without asking them. But this is the core of your strategy, the very first step you must take if you want to beat out the giants in your neighborhood. Will you balk at the first step? Or will you do it?

Need a little extra motivation to have that conversation? Soliciting feedback from your customers, believe it or not, is actually an excellent customer service practice. Think about the last time a business had this sort of conversation with you – probably a rarity! Knowing that your opinion really mattered would feel pretty good.

Once you identify exactly why people love doing business with you and the problem you really solve for them, you'll have your unique selling proposition (USP). In plain language, it means the unfair advantage you have in your marketplace, what separates you from everyone else. Your USP is the superhero power you have that none of your competitors can touch.

Once you've got that USP, your job is to hammer it home, pepper it throughout every piece of marketing you produce, and shout it from the rooftops. You'll feel like it's overkill after you hit that same point so many times – but about the time you're tired of saying it, your target clients will finally be hearing it for the first time. Your competitors – big and small – will give up on their USP long before you will. That's when the benefit of being a local provider of what you sell really takes off.

Your prospective customers, by and large, prefer to do business with someone local. In fact, your proximity and the fact that your business is locally owned rather than part of an impersonal multinational corporation is one way your small business actually has an advantage over your bigger competitors. Your USP differentiates you from all other options – and forms part of the story of your business. It's your story that hooks your ideal prospects. This is even more important than where you rank on the search engines!

Second, who do you most want to sell to?

You might think you'll sell your products and services to anyone with an open wallet. But that's probably not true. If you've been in business longer than 17 minutes, you can tell the difference between a great customer and a horrible one. If you're going to grow your business, why not grow it in the direction of serving even more of your greatest customers?

Before you unleash an onslaught of marketing tactics, it's worthwhile to identify these ideal customers so you can aim for more of them. Think about which customers are most profitable for you, which are most likeable, which have referred you to other great customers.

It's important to be disciplined in identifying these ideal clients, not just intuitive. In fact, if there were ever an ideal time to geek out and dig into your metrics, this is it. It works well to create a spreadsheet where you can rank your customers by the kinds of criteria that will help you understand – and ultimately replicate – your ideal customer.

Look for commonalities among your best customers. If you sell to consumers, consider their demographics (such as age, income, gender, education levels); if you sell to businesses look at firmographics (such as revenue, # of employees, their industries). This data creates your model. As you review each customer, ask yourself what would happen if your business had ten more just like this one – would you be more or less profitable, enjoy your business more or less, find working in your business easier or harder?

Talking with these customers helps you determine your true USP – but also helps you create a model ideal customer to replicate. Ask them how they'd go about finding other businesses like yours. Learn what they really think of you. You'll get a clear picture of what your key message should be, and which direction you should aim that message in order to grow your base of ideal customers. Your key messages have to be reflected in your website, your marketing collateral, and your customer service.

Consider your ideal customers' buying triggers

Pay attention to the psychographics (the mindset and the behaviors) of your ideal customers, too. Get a clear picture of who's ready to buy by understanding what's going on right before the point of sale.

For example, if you own an HVAC company, many of your new customers will call for service because their furnace just went out, leaving them shivering on a chilly day. Or, they're sweltering and dripping sweat, cursing out their air conditioner, which has just screeched to a halt on the hottest day of the summer. They'd rather never call you – but now they need you. They have an urgent problem you can fix, and they want to know that doing business with you will solve the problem quickly, without a hassle. They'll probably hire the first HVAC company that answers the phone and says a technician can come out immediately.

In contrast, let's say you own a jewelry store. Your customers probably do quite a bit of shopping around before buying. Impulse or rushed purchases might happen now and then, but it's going to be the exception. In general, your customers know they've got the luxury of deliberating a bit in the buying process. They're looking for evidence that you'll take good care of them, give them VIP treatment, and stand behind the quality of your goods – but they're happy to collect this evidence at a more leisurely pace, because they can just as easily not buy from you as buy.

Once you've nailed down the process and mental state that go with the purchase of your product or service, it's easier to identify which tactics will work best for you. You'll know where your ideal customers are, what media they consume, and what frame of mind they're in when they engage with you. You can tailor your tactics to how they'll respond best.

Become shiny object-proof

This valuable information will also protect you from being swayed by shiny objects presented by other business owners. You know how it goes. You're talking shop, and some guy starts bragging about the great results he's getting from the marketing tactic of the month. To hear him tell it, this new tactic he's trying is going to double or triple his business in the next 53 seconds. And it may be true – or it may not be. He may have stumbled onto a tactic that virtually explodes his business, but it still might not be a good fit for yours. It is easy to get confused by looking at other business owners' anecdotal evidence about certain marketing tactics and assuming these tactics will translate into more sales for you. Keep in mind that no two businesses are alike – an HVAC contractor's customers and a jewelry store's customers buy through very different channels and criteria, so what works for one business to attract customers may not work well for another.

Instead of jumping on marketing trends as they appear (and there's always a new one coming your way), it's important to understand what's really most likely to work for your business. Even if pay-per-click advertising is working well for one business, it may not be best for your business. You might find that your marketing sweet spot is in direct mail, event sponsorship, or some other tactic. With this information in mind, instead of investing your time and money in tactics that aren't effective, you'll have a roadmap for your marketing plan.

Your success depends on going with what's proven to work for your business. Get your strategy in place and then choose a few tactics to build your marketing plan.

In Duct Tape Marketing, we talk about the Marketing Hourglass™, which describes the seven steps needed for effective marketing.

This maps out the entire journey of a new customer finding you, doing business with you, and ultimately becoming one of your biggest fans. Many businesses – and probably your big competitors – focus their marketing mojo only on getting that first time purchase. They're missing out on some of the juiciest marketing fruit, which comes after your new customer buys the first time. How you work with your customers doesn't stop with the purchase. You want them to reactivate, renew, re-engage, and refer other ideal customers to you.

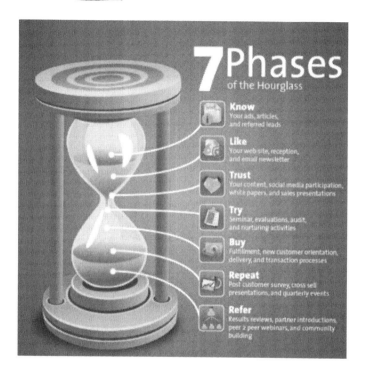

The well-thought-out marketing strategy should include at least one solid tactic for each of the seven phases: Know, Like, Trust, Try, Buy, Repeat, and Refer. Also, it's important to remember that this is not a static, one-and-done process – it's got to be revisited at least annually so you can constantly monitor how it's working and adjust so you can get increasingly better results over time.

Your strategy will help you build your complete marketing system. Systems are what enable any business to get predictable results. Once your marketing system is in place, you'll be able to dial it up at will to get more customers practically on command. That's an ideal position to be in, and one that even your biggest competitors can't touch.

How's that sound to you? Are you starting to see how, even if your competitors seem to have an unbeatable advantage over you as a locally owned business, you really CAN compete, and win?

Next up, you're going to learn how you can win the hearts, minds, and trust of your local customers and prospects using nothing but your words. In the marketing world, this is known as content marketing, and it's an absolute powerhouse when it comes to getting more ideal customers for your business. Content marketing is an opportunity for a local business to mop the floor with your bigger competitors and attract fiercely loyal customers.

⌘ ⌘ ⌘

Case Study: IT Services Provider

When you are targeting a specific geographic region with services that have a lengthy sales cycle, keeping your name in front of your target customers can be a challenge. And, in these situations customer references are usually critical to closing a sale.

We worked with The Computer Hut (www.comp-hut.com) to build and execute a program around gaining and publicizing positive customer case studies to use in multiple formats. The process is simple in design, though time-consuming in execution. We interviewed Computer Hut about how they position themselves in sales, how they differentiate themselves and why customers continue to do business with them for years. Then, we interviewed several of their best customers – asking the same questions. At the conclusion of the interviews we matched up the answers to determine where their most unique competitive strengths are and then based their marketing messages from that.

This work has been leveraged into content in many ways:

- Press releases announcing their new customer relationships with prominent companies in their service areas
- Web page and blog content
- Email newsletter content
- Social amplification through LinkedIn, Twitter and Facebook
- Marketing Kit material used in all Sales conversations
- Basis of a PR Campaign for Local Business Awards sponsored by statewide business journal

What this work has resulted in is increased press coverage, increased web traffic and most importantly increased inbound leads for the *company, which has enabled their sales force to more quickly qualify and advance sales opportunities instead of having to cold call to find new business. Now, leads "self-identify" as quality prospects for The Computer Hut because they already know that The Computer Hut can meet their needs from reading about how this work has been done for similar companies. Regular publication of customer case studies is now a core marketing strategy for The Computer Hut as it positions them way ahead of their competition who focus on capabilities in their communications (versus proven results). Additionally, the PR campaign that led to the company being a finalist for a statewide Business Of The Year Award also led directly to a quick-close sale as another finalist engaged The Computer Hut directly at the awards ceremony and had a sales meeting and proposal within two days.*

Mark Z. Fortune

www.fortunemarketinginc.com

⌘ ⌘ ⌘

Chapter Three: Out-Publish Them, Too

"When people show you who they are, believe them."

Maya Angelou

You've put up a website, have a well-established network in your area, and are an expert in your field. You have identified your ideal client and created a unique selling proposition that appeals to that ideal client. You know the buying triggers of your customers, and have a good idea of what motivates them and where to find them. You are now ready to jump into marketing tactics like direct mail, online advertising, referral programs, and social media… right?

Well… not quite. You see, before you begin pursuing marketing tactics that will drive potential customers to your doorstep (or virtual doorstep, in the case of a website), you have to have something for them to see once they get there. In the marketing world, that "something" can be summed up with one word: Content.

Yes, content. It is king, as you may have heard. Content is the first way you show people who you are. It's your foot in the door, your piece of their mindshare, your pathway through their minds and into their hearts. In other words, it is how you get someone who has never heard of your business to know, like, and trust you enough to do business with you.

The brand-name companies that you're competing against as a local business owner have figured this out. They're producing reams of content and using it to great effect, and if customers are comparison-shopping and don't see content from you, you won't get a second look. The good news is, producing your own content isn't as hard as you may think. You may not have an advertising budget that can compete with the big boys, but when it comes to content production, you can not only compete with them but also blow them out of the water. You'll learn exactly how to do that a little later in this chapter, but first let's take a deeper look at why content is so important.

What's The Point of Content, Anyway?

If you're like many new business owners, or even experienced business owners trying to take a new approach, one of the first questions on your mind when it comes to content marketing is… why? Isn't it better to leave the writing to the writers and focus on what you really do? Maybe. But that doesn't absolve you from needing to know what you need content-wise and then doing whatever it takes to get it produced and published.

See, content marketing isn't about writing for writing's sake. There's a whole strategy behind making content work to generate and nurture leads. You've got to actually show and tell people who you are if you want them to believe you enough to become your newest customers.

You might like to think that your brand-name competitor doesn't have the family values and local knowledge that you have – and you're probably right. But they're probably still pretty darned good at what they do. And if you let them broadcast their expertise while you sit back silently and wait for customers to come to you, your results will be disappointing – at best.

Think of your content this way: Imagine a prospective customer calls you up on the phone and is interested in doing business with you. They have a problem that you might be able to help them solve. Would you be willing to answer any questions that person had about your products or services? Would you be willing to tell them some stories about other people in similar situations you've been able to help? Would you share some details about yourself or your employees, and tell them about what their experience would be like if they worked with you? Would you be willing to give them a little bit of free advice, to demonstrate that you know what you're talking about? The answer to all of these questions is YES, YES, YES, a thousand times over—of course you'd be willing to do all of these things in order to close the sale!

Well, your content is simply something that will do this for you, twenty-four hours a day, three hundred and sixty-five days a year. And it will do it for people before they call your business. It will do it when they turn to internet search engines to get answers to their questions, because at their most basic level search engines are simply question-answering machines. Wouldn't you like to be the person who answers the questions your prospective customer has? Don't you think it's more likely that if you are that person (or that business, as the case may be), that it will be more likely that you'll earn their trust and get their business, if and when they are ready to buy?

The bottom line is this: a business card, pretty logo, and a nice tagline aren't going to help people find you online, they're not going to make them like you or trust you, and they're not going to close the sale. But content will.

What type of content do you need?

In order to accomplish all the goals we just mentioned, you'll need to have some very specific forms of content. At a minimum, you'll need the following:

- A case statement, which explains why someone needs your type of business to begin with
- A difference summary, or why you're different (and better) from the competition
- Your marketing story—how your business got started, and how it's grown over the years
- A list of products and services
- A description of your process
- Case studies about successful customers you've assisted
- Testimonials
- Frequently asked questions (FAQs)
- Should-ask questions (SAQs)

That last item on the list – SAQs – requires a little more explanation. Everybody knows what FAQs are – those are the questions that you hear all the time, and that you're almost sick of answering. But there are probably some questions that people never ask you, but that they really should ask you or any other company in your industry that they're considering doing business with. The only problem is, they just don't know enough about your industry to even know to ask those questions. By providing answers to those questions, you have the opportunity to really position yourself as an expert, and stack the deck in your favor. Your prospective customers are likely shopping around anyway – why not teach them how to do it in a way that ensures they end up back at your door when they're done? How many of your competitors educate customers about how to make a successful buying decision?

Once you've gathered all the types of content listed above, you can package it together in a marketing kit. Add some pictures, take it to your local printer, have a nice front and back cover designed, and print it as a booklet that you can hand out to prospective customers, strategic partners, and referral sources that will tell them everything they need to know about your business. This will blow your larger competitor's trifold brochure right out of the water, and really position you as a legitimate, professional business that deserves a closer look.

Of course, you don't have to call this document a "marketing kit". You could call it a "buyer's guide", "catalog", or "media kit", because it is actually all of those things. In fact, with a little bit of creativity, the marketing kit can form the foundation of your entire content marketing system.

Special Offer:

Visit localleadgenbook.com/special-offers to download a template for creating your marketing kit.

Repurposing and Reusing Your Content

Once you've invested some time creating the basic content listed above, you can begin getting more "bang for your buck" by re-using and re-purposing it. Begin by copying the content from each page of your marketing kit onto a page of your website. Your case statement and difference summary becomes the content for your home page; your marketing story becomes the "about us" page, and so on and so forth. Don't misunderstand us – there's a lot more that needs to go into a good small business website design than simply copying and pasting text, and we'll cover that in the next chapter. However, as far as the core written content for your website goes, your marketing kit will work just fine.

Next, take your list of 15-20 FAQs and SAQs and have one of your employees interview you on camera using those questions. Record each question and answer as a separate video, and keep your answers to no more than 1-2 minutes. Congratulations! You now have a video library to put on your company YouTube channel, embed on your website, or even use to create a DVD you can hand out to prospective customers (use a DVD duplication service to print copies with your company branding).

Now take your video library and send it to a transcription service like Rev.com to produce a transcript of each video. With a little bit of editing, you now have 15-20 blog posts for your website.

If you're feeling really ambitious, you can also use those blog posts as content for 15-20 monthly email newsletters, or turn those videos into 15-20 podcast episodes.

We've barely scratched the surface of how you can re-purpose your content. Here are some other ideas you might want to try:

- Use any two pages of your marketing kit—for example, your case study and FAQ page—to create a two-sided stand-alone flyer you can hand out at trade shows.

- Create a postcard you can use in a direct mail campaign using your difference summary on one side and your testimonials on the other (get a graphic designer to help you with the design).
- Use a PDF version of your buyer's guide (i.e., marketing kit) as a lead magnet in online advertising campaigns.
- Use your list of FAQs and SAQs to create a presentation that you can give in-person or online as a webinar.

See what we mean? With a little creativity, you will never have to create a one-and-done piece of content.

Get Strategic Partners Involved

Not only can you re-purpose your own content in a variety of ways, you can also use other people's content in your marketing efforts – and vice versa. We're not talking about stealing copyrighted material here. We're talking about strategic partners using each other's content with permission for the benefit of both parties.

In case you're not familiar with the term strategic partner, that refers to two businesses who serve the same target market but are not in competition with each other. For example, a pest control company and a lawn care company would both likely target middle-class homeowners as customers, but their services probably wouldn't overlap much, if at all. There are many ways that these companies can cooperate in their content marketing efforts. Here are a few examples:

- The lawn care company gives the pest control company a branded flyer to hand out to all their customers with tips about how to maintain a healthy lawn. In return, the pest control company gives the lawn care company a branded flyer to hand out to their customers about how to spot warning signs of termite activity.

- The lawn care company writes a guest blog post for the pest control company's website, and the pest control company reciprocates. Both companies link to each other's website and provide a little information about the other's business at the end of the blog post.

- The two companies join forces to produce a co-branded DVD or short e-book about how to maintain a lawn in a way that also reduces pest issues.

- Each company "sponsors" each other's monthly email newsletter with a specific call to action that is unique to that partner.

- Each business could list the other on a "trusted partners" page of their marketing kit, along with other strategic partners.

Of course, you'll want to make sure that the businesses you partner with can be trusted, since you'll be letting them borrow the trust you've established with your customers. We'll have much more about strategic partnerships in an upcoming chapter, but for now, we just want to make the point that content marketing can be a community effort.

Use Keywords in Your Content to Help it Get Found Online

Earlier in this chapter, we mentioned that one of the reasons to produce content was to help people find your business when they are searching for answers online. One way that you can make it more likely that your content will show up in relevant search results instead of your competitor's content is to use terms that people are likely to be searching for when you write your content. In online marketing lingo, these terms are called "keywords".

Luckily, you don't have to guess what these keywords might be. You can simply use a keyword planning tool, like the free tool provided by Google, to help you with your research (http://adwords.google.com/keywordplanner). If you don't want to take the time to learn how to use a new tool, you can do some quick-and-easy keyword research using the auto-complete feature of internet search engines – these are the words and phrases the search engine suggests as you type something in a search box. These can be a valuable source for keyword ideas to write content around, although they won't give you data about the number of searches being done for each term like the Keyword Planner will.

One important concept to be aware of – and take advantage of – when it comes to keywords is something called the "long tail effect". This basically refers to the fact that it will be very difficult for your local business to turn up in search results when someone searches for a very generic term, like "plumbers". There are millions of websites out there that use that term, and the likelihood that yours will show up on page one is virtually zero. However, if someone does a search for a more specific term – or in other words, one that has a longer tail – there is less competition, and thus more likelihood that your local business could show up. An example of a long tail search would be "residential plumber in Little Rock, AR". Well, if you happen to be a residential plumber in Little Rock, Arkansas, you would have a very good chance of showing up for that search – but only if you used those keywords in your online content.

We'll talk much more about keywords and how to get found online in an upcoming chapter, but we wanted to mention them here just in case you were so excited about getting started on your content marketing that you ran off to begin that process before you even finished the book. You see, you want to do your keyword research before writing your content, so that you can create a keyword list to use as you write. Keep the list handy as you create your content, and sprinkle the keywords in wherever you can.

Notice we said "sprinkle" – not "stuff". Internet search engines will actually punish businesses that try and cheat their way to the top of the search results by unnaturally stuffing keywords into their content. A good rule of thumb is that if it sounds strange to read, then you're probably using too many keywords. Let's take a look at another example using our friend the plumber from Little Rock, using some imaginary content from his website:

Too few keywords:

"All our customers agree that we're the best plumber around!"

Just the right amount of keywords:

"All our customers agree that Joe's Plumbing Service is the best residential plumber in Little Rock, AR!"

Too many keywords:

"All our Little Rock residential plumbing customers agree that Joe's Plumbing Service of Little Rock is the best residential plumber in Little Rock, AR."

You see what we mean? All three versions of the sentence above say essentially the same thing. However, the first version doesn't take advantage of long tail keywords, while the last version is something that is obviously written more for internet search engines than for a human reader. There was a time when tricks like that worked, but that time is long gone. Search engines have adjusted their algorithms, and when they see "keyword stuffing", they will punish the offending website by pushing it further down in the search results – or in extreme cases, banish it entirely.

How Should I Get Started with Content Marketing?

Now, you may be feeling a bit overwhelmed when you think about all the content you need to create, especially if you have a new business. If it feels overwhelming – simplify and prioritize; "chunk it down" to focus only on the areas of content you feel are most important, measure how it works and then adjust accordingly. The important thing is to get started – "perfect and in draft mode" loses to "good enough and done" every time.

Also, keep in mind that you don't have to do it all yourself. Do you have a team who can help you, or a designated writer that can take care of it? Should you accept that writing simply isn't your wheelhouse, and hire an outside copywriter?

Whether you're doing it yourself or hiring outside help, start by create a marketing kit using the formula mentioned above. Don't feel the need to complete every page just as listed; you can combine some of them if you like, and skip others if they really don't feel relevant to your business. But keep in mind that your marketing kit will form the foundation of your content plan for weeks, months, and even years to come, so some up-front investment in it now will pay off over the lifetime of your marketing plan.

Hopefully now you see that content marketing isn't some mystical process. Instead, it's a process of teaching people why they should work with you (or buy from you), building trust with them, helping them see how you're different from your competitors, and demonstrating that you can do what you say you can do. Your content helps your prospects trust that you're not just blowing smoke, that you really can help solve their problem.

Next up, we're going to talk websites. This might touch a nerve, but we figure you'd rather have the straight-up truth rather than the sugar-coated niceties your friends and family will give you to spare your feelings. Are you ready?

⌘ ⌘ ⌘

Case Study: Real Estate Investor Differentiated from the Pack

Rich Lennon is a real estate investor and owner of RVA Property Solutions in Richmond, VA (www.RVAPropertySolutions.com). When he first started his business, he was having difficulty distinguishing himself from all the other real estate investors trying to buy homes for cash, and as a result the only way he could compete was to pay more for the homes he was buying. To solve this problem, he started using a much more education-oriented approach in his sales process. He came up with a list of FAQs and SAQs, as well as checklists and assessments that homeowners could use to determine if selling for cash was their best option. He put all of this content in a marketing kit that he gives to homeowners when he visits their property to make an offer. His openness and honesty allows him to quickly build trust with homeowners, and thanks to that trust he is now often able to buy properties even when his offer is not the best one on the table.

Kevin Jordan
www.redpointmarketingconsultants.com

⌘ ⌘ ⌘

Chapter Four: Your Customers Are Looking for You - What Will They See?

"You'll never get a second chance to make a first impression."

Anonymous

Just like ripping off a Band Aid, there's a painful truth we've got to get out of the way here:

There's a good chance that your baby is ugly. And that baby is your website.

It's not your fault. It's not the end of the world. But you can't leave it like it is, and expect to compete against the big guys.

We know, the last thing you want to have to do is mess with your website again. How was your current site built? Did you pay someone (hopefully not your nephew… please tell us you didn't hire your nephew to build your site) good money to build your site? Did you get it in trade or as a favor from a friend or partner? Maybe you heard the promises of "drag and drop and get your business online this afternoon" ads from domain sellers or hosting services. Maybe you even installed a WordPress theme and tried to customize it.

Whatever the case, websites are not a "one and done" thing – they are the living, breathing home of your business online. And just like your physical home your online home needs consistent, high quality maintenance and improvements. If your website is doing absolutely everything for your business that you want and you are consistently ranked first on all of the search engine pages you want, great – just flip to the next chapter and pretend this little unpleasantness never happened. But if that little voice in your head is telling you that maybe your website isn't the lead generation powerhouse it could be, keep reading.

First, a Five-Second Test

First impressions matter, and more often than not a potential customer's first impression of you is your website.

And you've got to make that impression count quickly. You do NOT have a captive audience once you manage to get traffic to your website. They can just as easily click to your competitor's site as they can scroll through yours. In fact, studies have shown that people will decide within 5-8 seconds of arriving on a website whether to continue viewing more content on the site, or leave and check out a different site. Are you making the best possible impression and giving your visitors what they want and need in order to stay on your site long enough to get to know, like, and trust you?

Let's do a quick experiment so you can understand how prospective customers experience their first visit to your site. Choose a business that's not in your field – say, an automotive shop, HVAC company, or dentist. Do a quick Google search for that business type. Click on the fourth search result in the list. You've got 5 seconds to take a look, then you've got to close the site. Ready… GO!

Okay, time's up! Pencils down, please. Now think back to what you saw.

• Where was the company's phone number?

• Where was that business located?

• Where would you have clicked to find more information to schedule service?

Think also about how the site looked to you. Was it designed in a way that made being there a pleasant experience? Or, did you feel like it was assaulting your senses? The appearance is crucial to a website's performance… but looking good isn't everything.

Rhyme and Reason

Do you know what the difference is between a site that just looks pretty and one that looks good and also works like a beast to get new business for you? Strategy! No surprise there, right?

If you think about the last time you walked into a retail store like Wal-Mart or Barnes and Noble, what was the first thing you saw when you passed through the entrance? Carts, probably, maybe a greeter, possibly some sale items. As you walked through the store, what did you see? How about when you went to the check-out, what was right there within reach? Everything on the end caps, every item on shelves, even the heights of the shelves… all planned. In fact, these details are not just planned; they are strategized at great expense. The retailers know that this detailed planning for their layout will pay off big time because it capitalizes on human psychology and uses it to get people to buy more. There's a lot of psychology involved in how people act and shop online as well. There's a way they look at web pages. There are types of content they like – and don't like, and ways it's presented that encourage or discourage consumption and action. Every color, font, image, column, and every single detail of your site will either drive sales or repel them.

Investment or Expense?

So, how do you view your website? Is it an income-producing investment that works hard for you? Or, is it a necessary expense that gets funded begrudgingly, and one you'll spend the very least amount possible on to cross off your to-do list?

Here are some ways you can let your current website tell you which side of the fence you fall on here:

Wasted Traffic?

If you spend even a dime on generating website traffic – or even a dime on offline marketing materials – and your website isn't purposefully designed to attract, engage, and convert customers, you wasted that dime. We've seen it more times than you'd believe: A business owner spends a jaw-dropping amount of money on advertising that ultimately leads prospects to a site that isn't updated and doesn't reflect the same message as the advertising. What a waste of money! No matter what other marketing and advertising you're doing, all roads lead to Rome. Your website will make or break you. Your site is the center of all of your marketing. It impacts the success of your referrals, direct mail, reviews, and every other type of marketing you might ever try.

Too Hands-Off?

Some business owners simply refuse to invest in their websites. Some don't even claim their own domain names! They'll have a graphic designer or web developer do it for them – or that nephew we already discussed. This person buys the domain, throws a site up onto it, and then can't be found again – and now you're out of luck. Getting control of that domain name again is going to be challenging at best, and VERY expensive or even impossible at worst. It's almost a guarantee, if a business owner doesn't have control over the domain name, that they also don't have their own hosting plan – another huge mistake. You'd never think of buying a house and then letting your realtor put his or her name on the deed – and yet so many business owners make this exact mistake with their business domain name. Make absolutely sure you buy and maintain control of your business domain, and that you host your site on a hosting plan you pay for and have access to. This is the only way to ensure that you retain control of your site, no matter who you've got working on it for you. This way, if they flake out on you, you're not up the creek.

Drag & Drop Dud?

Maybe you heard an ad on the radio or saw one on TV. It promised you could build a great website for your business just by dragging and dropping a few ready-made elements in a template. You followed the call to action, and checked out the sample sites they displayed. Wow… looks great! So you fell for it. Of course, your site doesn't quite look like the example, but it looks good enough to you. The problem is that these sites, while very inexpensive to create, have just about zero strategy and search engine optimization built in. It's impossible to use a template drag and drop site to build the kind of website that can compete with what your competitors have. The search engines don't like these kinds of sites, and don't take your business seriously if you use them. Your potential customers aren't likely to have any better opinion, either. A site like this might be better than nothing, but really it's nothing better than an online digital brochure.

SEO? Ohhhhhh Yeah, Forgot about That.

Many businesses figure that if their website looks good, it is good. Maybe sometime after they build and launch the site they figure out that it's not actually showing up well in the search engine results. They're not getting any more phone calls or customers coming in than they had before they had a website.

Think of your website like a high-performance racecar. Performance should be built in from the start – not added on as an afterthought. It should be gorgeous to look at (design), built for speed (search engine optimization), and driven by a highly-skilled driver (marketing strategy). This is how you compete online with big competitors. You make sure your site is built to win. Your website is the hub of all of your marketing activities, and determines how well everything else you do to promote your business will perform. For it to perform well, you've got to begin to see it as an investment. In fact, the right website will actually provide a sweet return on income; every dollar you spend should bring back friends… right through the front door of your website.

An effective website is like the best employee you will ever have. Your website works 24 hours every day of the year. It never gets sick. It never needs personal time. It never complains. And after you have it up and running correctly, it doesn't cost you much at all to keep in place perpetually.

It doesn't matter if you are marketing a product, service or information, you have to be able to display what you have to offer - and you have to have it come off as top-of-the-line trustworthy. Especially for small businesses that are in competition with bigger, better-funded companies, it's imperative to make lasting impressions on new prospects.

If It's an Investment, Do What Counts

No matter how much money you can allocate toward your website, there are better and worse solutions available. Your website will never truly be complete – it will always be improving and growing, and shifting in response to changes in the search engines' algorithms. You can always take the next step to improve its performance, even if it means saving up first to take your site to the next level.

So, how do you get the kind of website you need to compete?

Strategy First, Of Course

You can't build a high-performance website by chance. It's not going to build itself – and without substantial planning and legwork, your website is more likely to be what we call a Frankensite than a sleek and powerful online lead generation machine. In this, you've got an advantage over some of your bigger competitors who've added on and expanded their websites without a plan for years and years. Like a sprawling farmhouse that's undergone one addition after another, they may have continuity and speed issues as well as an inability to adjust quickly to changes in what the search engines want to see in a site. You can do this right from the start, and take the lead!

Your site should reflect all the strategizing we've suggested so far in this book. Even with all the cool bells and whistles, and even if you dump a boatload of money into the development of your website, if you forget to build your site around your unique selling proposition, aimed at your ideal customer, and using the words your prospects will use to try to find you – you could end up with a great-looking site that can't be found or sends the same bland message as your competition. That's a complete waste. Put the time and effort into planning first, rather than just diving right into the building phase.

Every element of your website, from the graphics and content to the keywords and navigation, should be planned before you build. We'll talk more about SEO later, but you want to be sure you've got a plan for making your website search engine optimized before you start, too. You'll want to research and then use your best keywords, the right way and in the right places, to give your site the best chance of winning favor with the search engines.

Don't Propose Marriage on the First Date

Also, be sure every page on your website includes a call to action so your visitors can take the next logical step toward doing business with you. You don't want to level jump in the budding relationship you have with your prospective customers. Just lead them to the next, small step they should take to get what they need. If you hit them right away with BUY! BUY! BUY! It's a lot like popping the question on a first date – too soon, way too pushy, and sort of creepy. Instead, use strategic calls to action to make it a no-brainer step to walk further into your sales funnel. Don't make them guess what they should do next – and don't give them so many options or directions that they freeze in a state of overwhelm.

Make Sure You Can Reach Them Wherever They Are

Your prospects are very likely to visit your website on a mobile device. One of the most important features your website must include is that it's responsive. This simply means that it's easy to read and use on just about anyone's screen, from phone to desktop and everything in between. A responsive site will morph itself to fit any device. It loads quickly and never makes your visitors pinch and zoom in order to read the text or navigate. Do NOT get a separate mobile site in addition to your 'regular' site. That's an old solution for the mobile challenge, and it will work against you. Increasingly search engines punish sites that are not mobile responsive, so this is not an optional activity.

The Tools You Need

The good news is that today there are many ways to build a good, professional, high performing website without having to break the bank on a custom coded website or without suffering the shortcomings of the "drag and drop duds" we mentioned earlier. The authors have worked extensively with small businesses on website design, build and maintenance for years. We strongly recommend making sure your site is built on a Content Management System (CMS) platform that enables you (or your staff) to fully manage the site once it's built. And for most of the small businesses we work with we recommend using WordPress as that CMS. WordPress currently powers nearly 23% of all websites so there are significant robust tools and resources available for support and there is a large ecosystem for delivering new capabilities to WordPress-powered sites. (source: http://www.wpbeginner.com/why-you-should-use-wordpress/)

Your Site Could Be the Rainmaker

There are many WordPress-centered website platforms in the market. One of our favorites comes from a company called Copyblogger who has been a pioneer in content marketing from the very beginning. Their newest website platform is called Rainmaker. It's a fantastic tool with a lot of potential, and it's becoming enormously popular because of the powerful features it includes. To make Rainmaker perform to its fullest potential it is worth considering working with a good search engine optimization consultant who really understands the nuances of SEO for local businesses to make sure your site has what it needs to get positive attention from the search engines.

Here's a quick laundry list of what Rainmaker includes:

- Secure web hosting
- Website creation software
- Landing page creation software
- Podcasting hosting and distribution tools
- Responsive and HTML5-compatible theme software
- Search Engine Optimization software
- A/B testing software
- Shopping cart software (you will need a merchant account like Stripe, Authorize.net, Braintree, or PayPal)
- Affiliate software
- Membership site software
- Forum software

It's a robust, high-performance platform that runs all sorts of tools to help you build and maintain the kind of web presence you need to compete against the big guys. Any one of us can help you use this powerful tool to build the kind of website we've been discussing.

In fact, if you'd like a free website assessment, just ask and one of us will be happy to give your existing site a close look and then provide you with some recommendations based on your budget. Our goal is to help you make the most out of your website development budget so you get the biggest impact for the smallest investment possible.

Special Offer:

Visit localleadgenbook.com/special-offers to download an infographic showing you exactly how to design a local business website for best lead conversion and search engine optimization results.

Coming up next, it's time to talk about two three-letter terms that could lead you down an endless rabbit trail of research if you wanted to learn all there is to know. Don't worry, though, we'll make it painless and profitable for you to learn what you need to know about SEO and SEM.

⌘ ⌘ ⌘

Case Study: Local ATV Dealer Becomes #1 through AdWords & Effective Website

We were helping a local ATV dealer that operated out of a smaller mountain town in California. They had a small marketing budget and

*wanted to advertise their ATVs online using Google AdWords over a
wide area in order to get more business. Very few dealers have any
luck with this approach because people will just buy from a local dealer
that is closer to them.*

*So instead of focusing on the actual ATVs, we focused on the
uniqueness of this dealer and his location. Being in the mountains he
could help people find good trails to ride and organize group trips to
riding areas and overnight camping. With this unique focus, this dealer
was able to pull in buyers from as many as two hours away driving in
from the bay area who purchase from them and become a part of the
"team".*

*This dealership became the #1 selling Polaris dealer in Northern
California beating out larger dealerships with bigger budgets in the Bay
Area by using a simple AdWords campaign and affordable but
differentiated website that told the right story. They have very little
competition for their AdWords clicks and pay under $1 for most of the
clicks they receive.*

Justin Sturges
www.systemadik.com

⌘ ⌘ ⌘

Chapter Five: Using Internet Search to Generate Leads

"If it isn't on Google, it doesn't exist."

Jimmy Wales

Co-founder of Wikipedia

We've spent a lot of space in this book discussing some very old-school methods of lead generation—direct mail, referral marketing, public speaking, and so on. Those tried-and-true methods are still very important and effective, and should be a part of your marketing plan.

However, it's now time to turn our attention to two subjects that, for many local small business owners, are very new and very foreign: search engine optimization and search engine marketing, better known in the marketing world as SEO and SEM. Simply put, SEO and SEM are how potential customers who need your products and services will find you instead of your competitors when they turn to the Internet for answers—as the overwhelming majority of them now do.

The fact is that the Jimmy Wales quote at the beginning of this chapter could easily be re-worded to read: "If you aren't on Google, you don't exist"—at least in the minds of most of your prospective customers. What that means to you is that even if SEO and SEM aren't your favorite topics, you as a local small business owner can't afford to ignore them.

While you don't need to become an expert, you need to have at least a basic understanding of what they are and how they work. Our goal in this chapter is to give you that basic understanding so that you can communicate intelligently if you hire experts to help you with this area of your marketing—which is something we strongly recommend that you do. If we compared building your lead generation system to building a house, doing your own SEO and SEM would be like doing your own electrical wiring (assuming you're not an electrician)—the consequences of getting it wrong are just too big and too expensive not to bring in a professional.

Ok, so you understand that this stuff is important…but what exactly are SEO and SEM?

A Brief History of SEO and SEM

Once upon a time, Internet search engines like Google, Yahoo, and Bing were created to help people find content online. These search engines send out "spiders", which are basically programs that "crawl" the Internet and index all the content it contains. When someone does a search online, the search engines use algorithms to determine which content is most relevant to the search being done, and present that content to the person doing the search in order from most relevant to least relevant.

Shortly after the creation of Internet search engines, website owners quickly discovered that adhering to certain best practices made it much more likely that their sites would turn up first when someone did a search related to what their websites were about. We'll get into what exactly those practices are later in this chapter, but for now, just understand that the process of applying those best practices became known as Search Engine Optimization or SEO for short. Before long, a whole industry cropped up around helping website owners apply these practices. In fact, if you've been in business for any length of time you've probably been contacted by someone trying to sell you SEO services - more on that shortly.

Now, anytime that the demand for something exceeds the supply, there is money to be made, and that's the case with Internet search as well. You see, there are only a limited number of spots on the first page of search results--and most people don't look beyond that first page of results. The demand from companies who would like to be included at the top of search results far exceeds that limited supply. Search engines make their money—lots of it—by reserving a select number of spots in the search results for companies who pay to advertise there. The process of paying to show up in search results is known as Search Engine Marketing. It's sometimes referred to as Pay-Per-Click advertising or simply PPC, because participating companies don't pay until someone actually clicks on their ad.

What's in a Name?

Even within the marketing industry, there's a lot of confusion about the terms SEO and SEM and what they each mean. Some people even use them interchangeably, while others use the term SEM to refer to all marketing activities related to Internet searches, including SEO. For the purposes of this book, we're going to use the term SEO to refer to the process of applying best practices to help your website turn up in the organic or non-paid search results, and we'll use the term SEM to refer to the process of using advertising to make your website appear in the paid search results.

Although SEO and SEM are distinctly different disciplines, each with their own rules and strategies, they are also intertwined in the sense that they both involve helping your website turn up in search results. As a result, your SEO and SEM efforts need to be closely coordinated in order to get the best results.

What's the Big Deal with Google, Anyway?

As soon as you start diving into the geeky world of SEO and SEM, you'll start to hear people talking a lot about Google. Sometimes it might seem as if Google makes the rules for the entire Internet. The fact is that search engines are the gatekeepers of the vast amount of content available on the Internet, and since Google is by far the largest search engine, they're the one you need to pay attention to. In fact, at the time of this book's publication, Google gets more traffic than the four next-largest search engines combined— over 1.1 billion unique visitors every month (those other search engines, by the way, are Bing, Yahoo, Ask, and AOL).

Each Internet search engine has their own top-secret algorithm that they use to determine which websites show up at the top of organic search results (SEO), and they each have their own advertising platforms that they use to sell top spots in the paid search results (SEM). However, for our purposes there really isn't much difference between Google and other Internet search engines other than the volume of traffic that they get. For the sake of simplicity, for the remainder of this chapter we'll focus our SEO discussion on the guidelines published by Google, and we'll focus our SEM discussion on Google's AdWords advertising platform. If you understand the basics of those, by default you'll also understand how other search engines work as well.

It Starts with Keywords

As you may remember from the chapter on content marketing; a keyword is simply something that someone types into a search engine when they do a search. Even though we use the term keyword to describe it, a keyword could actually be a phrase, like "residential pest control" or "commercial alarm systems". They're at the heart of both SEO and SEM, because before you begin to do either one you need to know what keywords people might be using to search for YOUR business.

As we described previously, there are several easy-to-use (and free) tools available to help you come up with a list of potential keywords, most notably Google's own Keyword Planner tool. Simply start by typing a phrase into the tool that you think people might use to search for you, and the tool will give you a list of related keywords along with data about how many searches are done for each term every month. It will also tell you how competitive each term is—in other words, how many other websites are trying to show up at the top of search results for that term.

You'll notice that shorter, less descriptive terms have much more competition than longer terms. This is the long tail principle we described earlier in the chapter on content marketing, which states that the more descriptive a keyword is, the easier it will be for your website to show up when people search for it. The great news for local businesses is that over 40% of all searches done on Google use a "local" long-tail keyword—for example, "HVAC service Roanoke VA". That means that by using the names of the cities, counties, and even specific neighborhoods that you serve in your SEO and SEM efforts, you can dramatically increase their effectiveness.

Once your keyword research is complete, you should have a list of several hundred potential keywords that people might use to search for your business. This may seem like a lot, until you consider all the possible ways people might describe what you do. For example, a keyword list for our imaginary Roanoke, Virginia-based HVAC company might start like this:

Roanoke VA HVAC Service

Roanoke VA HVAC Company

HVAC Repair Roanoke VA

Roanoke VA HVAC maintenance

Residential HVAC Ronoke VA

Commercial HVAC service Roanoke VA

Residential HVAC repair Roanoke VA

Commercial HVAC company Roanoke VA

Roanoke VA Commercial HVAC repair

Roanoke VA HVAC repair service

That's ten keywords just using variations on the words Roanoke, VA, and HVAC. We haven't even started getting into variations using terms like air conditioning, heating, heat pumps, furnace, etc. We can also add variations referencing specific geographic localities near Roanoke, like Cave Springs, Vinton, and Salem. You can see how your keyword list can quickly grow to several hundred terms when you start using all these possible combinations.

Now that you have at least a basic list of keywords, let's discuss how you can put that list to use in your SEO and SEM efforts.

On-Page SEO

SEO can be broken down into two categories—on-page SEO and off-page SEO. On-page SEO has to do with all of the content on your website, from the text content and media, to the structure and layout, and the coding that binds it all together. Since you have total and complete control over your own website, we'll start there.

There are many factors that search engines use to rank your website. In fact, Google has stated that they use over 200 different factors in their ranking algorithms – way too many to cover in a chapter of this book. For an on-page SEO example, let's start with a basic ranking element that everyone understands: keywords. For each page of your website, you'll want to pick one or two main keywords that you really want that page to show up for in search results. When you write the content for that page, make sure to include the keywords in several locations, especially in main headings or sub-headings of different sections on the page. It is important to work your targeted keywords into the content in a natural, well-written way.

You'll also want to make sure that your main keyword for the page is included in the URL, the title tag, the meta tag, and in alt descriptions used for images on the page. A full definition of those terms is beyond the scope of this chapter; so if you don't know what any of those things are, just go to www.LocalLeadGenBook.com/resources for an explanation.

Another thing you'll want to do is selectively create anchor text links using your target keyword and put them on other pages of your website linking to the page in question. Only do this on pages where it adds editorial value and don't just shoehorn them in for SEO. An anchor text link is a link where you can click the actual text to go to the link instead of clicking on a URL. For example, if we told you to visit www.LocalLeadGenBook.com/resources   for   a   full explanation of anchor text links, that would not be an anchor text link. However, if we told you to visit the Local Lead Generation book website and made the words "Local Lead Generation book" a clickable link, that would be an anchor text link (of course, we can't do that in a paper book…at least, not yet). Aside from cross linking to pages within your website, it can also be helpful to your visitors and the search engines if you include outbound links to high authority third party websites that add editorial value to the page content.

You'll need to repeat this process for each and every page of your website. You'll also want to do it every time you create a new page, such as a blog post. As you can imagine, if you have a website with many pages, this can quickly become rather complicated and time-consuming—which is one of the reasons we recommend hiring a professional to assist you with it. You'll also want to keep in mind that

Google has very detailed rules and guidelines with respect to on-page SEO, you can read more at: https://support.google.com/webmasters/

Off-Page SEO

The second category of SEO has to do with what's called "off-page" factors. Some of these factors you can control, some you can influence, and some you have no control over whatsoever. Really, what off-page SEO boils down to is how strong of a referral the Internet gives to your website. Think of it like this: imagine you ask ten friends to recommend a good dentist. Four of your friends strongly recommend Dentist A, two of them give a lukewarm recommendation for Dentist B, and the other four all recommend different dentists. Which dentist are you most likely to pay attention to? For most of you, it's probably Dentist A.

In a sense, Google is like someone asking their friends for a recommendation, only Google's "friends" are all the websites on the entire Internet. When someone does a search, Google checks the Internet to see which of the websites relevant to their search are most "recommended" by the rest of the Internet. Those websites with the best on-page and off-page SEO will then be displayed first in the search results.

Google collects many types of off-page signals to rank your website. One of the most important is backlinks - that is a clickable link from a third party website that points back to your site. The location of the link on a web page, the type of link (i.e. an anchor link vs a linked image vs a plain URL) and the text around the link all affect the SEO value of a given link. There are other off-page ranking factors as well, such as social engagement. When you post a new blog article on your website, and the article gets liked and shared and inspires discussion and comments, these are emerging ranking factors that Google is using more and more as an off-page ranking signal.

A word of caution: Because backlinks are still a very important ranking factor, they are also the most scrutinized by the search engines. Google has strict guidelines on backlinks and very specific technologies designed to filter and penalize websites that try to acquire backlinks for the sole purpose of manipulating search results. On the other hand, you do need to make an effort to get backlinks from high-quality websites that are relevant to your business.

What do we mean by high-quality, relevant links? Well, in the same way that you respect the opinions of some of your friends more than others (just admit it—we know it's true), Google respects some websites more than others, and is more likely to pay attention to their recommendations. The funny thing is that both you and Google probably use the same criteria when determining whose recommendation to listen to. You probably tend to listen to and respect friends who are older, wiser, and highly respected by lots of other people, right? Well, Google "respects" the recommendation of websites that have been around a while, have lots of high-quality content, and are perceived to be an authority in their niche. Your goal is to try and get as many of these sites as possible to naturally link to your website.

So, what kind of websites are we talking about here? Here are some typical examples that would apply to most local businesses:

- Your local Chamber of Commerce website
- Online directories and review sites (see the chapter on reputation management)
- Industry associations or trade group websites
- Websites of local non-profit organizations
- Social media sites
- Local government websites
- University, college, and other official school websites
- Websites for local media (newspapers, radio, TV news, etc.)
- Websites of other well-established local businesses (via guest blogging)

Now, your next question is probably going to be, "How do I get those websites to link back to my site?" This is where it gets a little tricky, because it really depends on the individual websites. For social media sites and most online directories, it's simply a matter of you taking the time to create or claim a profile on those sites and adding a link back to your site. For the websites of local chambers of commerce or industry groups, it will probably require you to (gasp) actually be a member of those organizations (which, let's face it… you probably should be).

When it comes to getting links from the websites of other local businesses, nonprofit organizations, and the media, it really comes down to good old-fashioned networking. You have to establish relationships with local reporters, build rapport with other business owners, and actively participate in your community. In other words, you need to do all the stuff you really should be doing anyway as a local business owner.

One thing you can do to encourage more people to link back to your site is to regularly publish high-quality, useful information. If you're a CPA, for example, write a blog post about the top five mistakes most people make when filing their taxes. It's a lot more likely that people would link to that than a page that simply has a bullet-point list of the services you provide.

Remember the marketing kit from the chapter on content, and how we discussed creating lists of frequently asked questions, should-ask questions, and case studies? That's the type of content that will generate high-quality backlinks.

Of course, in order for people to link back to your content, they have to know it exists. You can make your content easier to find by sharing it on your social media platforms, and adding social media sharing buttons to your website to encourage other people to share it. You can also mention it in your email newsletter, tell your strategic partners about it, promote it in your direct mail campaigns, and use it in your live events. If we're doing our job, a light bulb should have just turned on in your head as you realize we just tied together everything we talk about in this book. If so, that means you're finally starting to get the fact that all these tactics, including SEO, work best when they work together!

As you're probably starting to realize, good SEO–both on-page and off-page—is not a one-and-done proposition. Ideally, you (or the professional you hire to assist you with your SEO) should review your efforts on a monthly basis to see how you're doing. Use your Google analytics report and Google webmaster tools data to help you determine what keywords people are using to find your site and where you rank in the search results for each keyword (visit localleadgenbook.com/resources for more information about these tools). That way you'll know what keywords to focus on as you produce new content (like blog posts) for your website.

For many local small business owners, staying on top of this task is difficult if not impossible without outsourcing at least some of the work. Unfortunately, outsourcing your SEO to the wrong person can have catastrophic results, so we'd like to spend a quick minute discussing how to tell the difference between a good SEO professional and a bad one.

White Hats and Black Hats

Anytime that a system for something exists, there are people who will try and cheat the system, and such is the case with the world of Internet search. These cheaters are known in the marketing world as "Black Hat SEO" types. Their approach is to try and trick the search engine algorithms into ranking a website at the top of search results that really has no business being there—in essence, taking advantage of loopholes. Remember our discussion about "keyword stuffing" from the chapter on content marketing, using the example of Joe's Plumbing Service from Little Rock? That's a classic black hat SEO tactic. Other common black hat tactics include:

- Buying links—in other words, paying websites for backlinks instead of attempting to get high-quality backlinks using the techniques we described above.
- Article spinning—taking one piece of content, making minimal changes to it, and publishing it in numerous places with links back to your site.
- Hidden text or links—putting links on a website that are invisible to a human reader (i.e., white text on a white background), but that can be read by a search engine's spiders.

There are many more black hat SEO tactics, but those are some of the most-used (or should we say, abused). While these tactics may work in the short term, as soon as the search engines catch on to what the black hat types are up to, they make changes to their algorithm to close the loopholes. If the SEO professional you hire is relying on these tactics to get traffic from Internet search results to your website, you will see a large drop-off in that traffic when the loopholes are closed. In extreme cases, these tactics could even get your website banned from even appearing in Google search results at all.

So, how can you avoid these black-hat SEO people? Here are some red flags to look for:

- Avoid people who "guarantee" that if you work with them you will have top rankings in Google.

- Avoid people who cold-call or autodial your business claiming to be from Google, informing you of a problem with your listings. Google does not call businesses—this is just a scare tactic.

- Avoid working with people who present you with a long-term SEO plan that does not include any ongoing production of content.

The bottom line is that you should use the same process when you hire an SEO professional as you do with any other employee or vendor—ask for references, check their reviews and testimonials, and do your due diligence.

Where Does SEM Fit In?

Ok, so we've given you a basic understanding of SEO and all that it entails. Hopefully your eyes haven't started to glaze over too much, because we still need to cover the second way that you can help customers find you using Internet search—SEM, also known as paid search or Pay-Per-Click.

While SEO is more of a long-term process that can take weeks or even months to start yielding results, SEM is something that can start sending traffic to your site immediately—even tomorrow. Unfortunately, many business owners falsely believe that just because it can be set up and turned on fairly quickly, paid search advertising is an easy way to get new customers.

The truth, as usual, is a bit more complicated. While an in-depth discussion of SEM is beyond the scope of this book, as with SEO we want to give you a basic understanding of the subject so that you can at least ask the right questions.

How Does Pay-Per-Click Advertising Work?

Basically, paid search advertising on Google works like this: advertisers (that's you) sign up for a free account on Google's advertising service, AdWords (www.google.com/adwords). They submit a list of keywords they'd like to target, and create ads related to the keywords. Finally, they specify how much they'd be willing to pay if someone were to click on one of their ads. This is known as "bidding" on a keyword.

Every time someone does a search on Google, AdWords holds an auction. It checks to see how many companies, if any, have bid on the keyword used in the search, as well as how much those companies bid. It will then display the ads from the top bidders in the search results, typically at the top of the page and on the right-hand side of the screen.

Now, here's the part that makes search advertising unlike any other form of advertising: if nobody clicks on a company's ad after it is displayed in the search results, that company pays nothing. The business only pays if someone clicks on its ad in order to learn more (typically when clicked the ad will link to the business's main website or to a special one-page website called a landing page set up specifically for the ad). This is where the term Pay-Per-Click advertising comes from.

The amount an advertiser has to pay for the click is determined by how much competition there is for the keyword that triggered the ad to appear. The cost can be anywhere from a few cents to over $10. Businesses that sell high-priced products or services can expect to pay more for clicks, as can businesses in industries where the lifetime value of a customer is very high (insurance, financial services, automotive sales, real estate, etc.). Businesses with lower-priced products or services, such as hair salons or car washes, will pay less.

The Devil Is in the Details

In addition to specifying how much they want to pay for a click and what keywords they want to bid on, businesses can use a wide variety of other criteria to determine how and when their ads appear. Here's a partial list of criteria that can be used in ad targeting:

- Geographic location: Businesses can choose to have their ads appear only for people doing searches within a certain radius of their location. Cities, states, counties, zip codes, and even congressional districts can also be used in geographic targeting of ads.

- Type of device: Advertisers can decide whether they want their ads to appear only for people doing searches on desktop and laptop computers, or only on mobile devices, or both.

- Time of day and day of the week: Businesses can choose to have their ads appear only when they are open, or only on weekdays or weekends.

Another criteria advertisers can use is keyword match. Companies can choose to have their ads appear only when the search term used exactly matches a specified keyword, or they can have their ads appear for the keyword plus related terms. The latter option is known as a broad match. For example, an exterminator who bid on the keyword "pest control" using the broad match criteria would also have his ads show up if someone searched for "termite control" or "wildlife control".

This is where Pay-Per-Click advertising can start to get a little tricky. When you come up with a list of keywords to bid on, you're basically trying to guess the intent of people searching for those keywords. You only want to target people who are searching with the intent to buy your product or service, but this can be difficult at times. For example, you might think that someone searching for "pest control" would be interested in hiring a pest control company. However, that person could be looking for a job in pest control, they could be interested in learning how to do their own pest control, or they could be researching the safety of chemicals used in pest control. If you owned a local pest control business, you wouldn't want any of those people clicking your ads, because if they did you'd be wasting your money.

In fact, if you don't know what you're doing, there are many ways you can waste money on Pay-Per-Click advertising. In addition to all of the targeting criteria listed above, there are lots of other factors that will determine the success or failure of an AdWords PPC advertising campaign, such as ad copy, landing page design, and ad quality score.

There is so much to learn about this topic that Google has even created a certification program for professionals who want to help small business owners with their PPC advertising. The authors of this book highly recommend that you work with one of these professionals if you are interested in testing paid search advertising as a means of generating leads. If you'd like to work with one of us, you can visit www.leadgenbook.com/resources to request a free consultation, or you can visit www.google.com/partners/ for a complete list of all Google certified partners.

Put on Your Running Shoes

Have you ever heard the joke about the two men running away from the bear in the woods? As the bear gains on them, one man suddenly stops to change into running shoes. The other man asks him, "What the heck are you doing—you'll never outrun the bear if you stop now!" The first man replies, "I don't have to outrun the bear—I only have to outrun YOU!"

This is a good way to think of SEO and SEM for a local business. If you're feeling a little overwhelmed right now with all the information we've thrown at you in this chapter and all the tasks you have to do, just remember: In order for your SEO and SEM efforts to start paying off, you don't have to do it perfectly. You just have to do it better than your local competitors!

In most small to mid-sized markets, there will only be two or three businesses that are doing this stuff really well. The rest either won't be doing it at all, or will be making a very minimal effort. Even if all you do is create a keyword list and do some basic on-page SEO on your website, you'll already be ahead of half of your competitors. If you start publishing high-quality content on a regular basis using your keywords, and make an effort to get some quality backlinks to your site, within six months to a year you'll probably be dominating the local search results for your industry.

We've covered a lot of marketing tactics so far, so you're probably wondering how to know whether what you're already doing is "good enough" – and how to know what's working best, what should be scrapped, what could be tweaked… basically, how to know whether you're doing it right. We'll dive right into that when you turn the page.

⌘ ⌘ ⌘

Case Study: SEO – How David Beats Goliath Online

We have a client, Viral Video Marketing LLC (www.viralvideokc.com) in Kansas City, which is one of the metro area's leading video production and online video marketing companies. The owner, Christian Vedder, is an authority on online video marketing and more SEO-savvy than your average small business owner. Despite getting some good search engine optimization traction through his own efforts, Christian knew his search engine rankings could be better, so he sought out the help of a professional.

Through an SEO audit of his website, we found that by making a few technical adjustments and enhancing some of the content throughout the site, we were able to uncork a lot of ranking value that was essentially hidden from the search engines. Some of the changes included WordPress plugin configuration, text optimization and cleaning up a lot of website code from the previous developer. In short, we made it faster and a lot more Google-friendly.

We also coached Christian on implementing a proactive online reputation strategy and well as content marketing strategy that included highly targeted guest blogging. In just three short months, Viral Video Marketing gained dominant local search rankings; beating more established video production companies – and getting his phone to ring like never before.

Phil Singleton

www.kcseopro.com

⌘ ⌘ ⌘

Chapter Six: You May Be Small, But You Can Have Perfect Aim

"Measurement is the first step that leads to control and eventually to improvement. If you can't measure something, you can't understand it. If you can't understand it, you can't control it. If you can't control it, you can't improve it."

H. James Harrington

If you've put into place at least some of the suggestions from the last few chapters, then you now have the start of a pretty good system in place for marketing your local business and getting the attention of the people you'd most like to serve.

However, without accurate measurements for what's working and what isn't, chances are you're wasting time and money with some efforts that aren't really paying off, while you're missing the opportunity to amp up endeavors that are getting results. There is a common saying in marketing that only 50% of what you're doing is actually working… the trick, of course, is knowing which 50% that is. Most business owners and marketers don't bother trying to figure that out – so about half of their marketing resources are completely wasted.

Don't let that happen to you.

Instead, measure. Sure, you're probably already measuring the big things like revenue, profit and cash flow. But you should be measuring more than that. And yes, using analytics to track how each of your marketing efforts is doing involves a bit of a learning curve, but it is well worth it in the end. Once you start measuring your results, you'll be able to see:

- What works
- Who it's attracting
- Where they're coming from
- Which of your customers turn into repeat customers
- … and much more.

These stats will give you highly valuable information, such as what your perfect customer looks like (so you can continue to target him or her), where they spend most of their time (so you can start spending your marketing resources there to reach them), and what you can do to get their business again (or for life!). It all comes down to analytics.

So Just What Are Analytics?

The majority of business owners agree that marketing is important, yet according to a Content Marketing Institute Survey in 2014 only 21% are successful at tracking the return on their marketing investments (http://contentmarketinginstitute.com/2014/10/2015-b2b-content-marketing-research/).

Many aren't sure what to measure, how to measure it, and what to do with the information afterward, so let's break this down, starting with what, exactly, analytics are.

Small business owners are often confused when they hear the word "analytics." They usually associate it with online stats, such as bounce rates and other metrics that come with paying close attention to the performance of a website. While these tidbits are helpful to know, marketing analytics overall are much more comprehensive than simply web analytics.

Think of analytics as the collection of instruments on a car dashboard. If the car is your "marketing machine," your collective marketing effort comprises the dashboard. All of those instruments tell you where you rock and where you… well, need some work. Marketing analytics should evaluate every marketing effort you make as a business owner.

At a minimum, they must measure:

- Number of customers overall
- Number of new and repeat customers
- Average sales and profit from each customer or transaction
- Number of leads generated
- Percent of leads converted to sales
- Percent of sales that turned into repeat customers
- Percent of customers referring new customers

Not only should it measure more than the results of your website, a good marketing measurement plan will measure more than just the results of any single marketing endeavor, instead judging your efforts as a whole and providing valuable insight into which efforts work in combination. Advanced analytics can measure the results of several different marketing strategies working in concert.

For example, you might measure how many people on your email list open your email, click through to your website, and actually convert – meaning they purchase a good or a service. Or you might measure how many people on your site are coming from Facebook, and of those people, who converted. You can even use analytics to see which Facebook post they're coming from, so you can tell if a particular promotion or story does better than others.

Analytics, in other words, shouldn't be a scary word. Really it's just a fancy way of saying "awesome info to have," so don't let the terminology run you off. Instead, start gathering this information. If you've never tracked your efforts before and are intimidated, that's okay: start small, tracking one effort at a time, before moving on to others. Soon enough, you will build up a robust measurement plan that accounts for every marketing effort you make.

How to Gather Analytics

So just how should you gather the information you need? Although we've already discussed that marketing and web analytics are not the same thing, your website is still a great place to start. You can use web analytics to mine a lot of important data about your customers and their behavior. Use your website's analytics to get a handle on who is coming, where they come from, what they do on their site once they get there.

Don't focus simply on web traffic, though. When you are assessing your site's performance, things like page views and traffic are important; when you are looking at marketing analytics, you should focus on your prospects, customers, and their behavior. Look for patterns that can help you market more effectively next time.

For instance:

- Do you notice that Facebook traffic only ever results in customers who click around, then leave?
- Are you getting great results for a particular search term?
- Have you gotten fabulous results from a particular marketing offer?

Particularly valuable to know about is the point of conversion, or the actual moment when a consumer said, "Yes, let's do it!" and made the decision to become your customer. If you can figure out what triggered this behavior and set up your marketing plan so that it encourages that behavior for other prospects, then you can replicate the result and ditch the ho-hum efforts.

In addition to your website's analytics, the marketing world abounds with useful tools you can employ to gather more information on your customers. You can use these tools to harvest and record data on your website, your email leads, your social media success, even your analog efforts such as mailers.

If that feels too overwhelming, start much smaller in your data gathering efforts. Create a simple spreadsheet and capture the number of leads, number of customers, and the number of new customers versus number of repeat customers. Capture that information every month for three to six months. Then sit down and focus on the trends that are emerging.

What happened? What do you need to do differently? What will it take to get there? Just those simple steps will yield great insights to your business. To get started populating this spreadsheet, simply ask every new customer how they heard about you when you first engage them, this will either prove or disprove your current "gut instinct" marketing planning. Also, install Google Analytics on your website (great instructions at www.google.com/analytics). This will give you great insight on how to improve your web marketing efforts.

The next level of analytics begins with using Customer Relationship Management (CRM) systems to help you organize all the data you're collecting. These are software programs specifically designed to help you keep track of everything we've been discussing in this chapter. Some of the more powerful CRM systems even combine other marketing functions like email marketing, social media marketing, and direct mail marketing in one platform. There are many CRM systems on the market, but some that the authors recommend include Zoho, Infusionsoft, and Nimble, which are mainly built for the needs of small businesses.

Remember, what gets measured gets acted on. If you do not know which efforts are producing (or are not producing) results for your business then you will find yourself guessing as to what to do next and growing increasingly frustrated with the whole effort. Avoid that fate by gathering analytics and then putting them to work for you.

How to Put Your Sales and Marketing Analytics to Work

Your goal with marketing analytics is to ditch the efforts that are wasting your time and play up the ones that are working really well. Often your marketing analytics will give you a really clear picture of how you're doing through comparison, such as:

- Comparing results to other results in similar time frames so you can chart your progress, hopefully seeing growth over time

- Comparing the results from one endeavor (email) to another (direct mail) to see how they stack up
- Comparing results from different customer segments, such as new and repeat customers

When you can easily compare results, you can see where your marketing machine needs a tune-up, and can begin to fine-tune your marketing efforts with ever-greater accuracy and results.

How, you're wondering? Let's say you have a lead-generation effort that normally produces great results, but when your leads call on the phone rather than coming through your website, they tend to get lost and no conversion occurs. Once you know this, you can look for an answer: Is your staff poorly equipped? Is your phone system too cumbersome? Is it too hard to get what they need over the phone? You can then correct these issues, resulting in the likelihood of more sales via this marketing channel.

This is just one example, of course, but it highlights an important point: When you can figure out why something isn't working – which admittedly may take some work – you can correct glitches in your system, act on them, and measure whether or not the problem has been fixed.

Voilà: a more responsive marketing machine.

Fine-Tuning the Marketing Machine

Once you get to a point of comfort with your marketing process, you can add on. Ask yourself questions such as:

- Who in the company is responsible for following up with leads, and do they have everything they need to create conversions?
- How can you advance leads down the path to conversion?
- How can you turn a customer into a repeat customer?
- How can you encourage referrals?
- Can you make working with you a more pleasant experience somehow?
- Can your customers pay easily at the point of service?
- Do you offer a Welcome Kit that helps your customers better understand your service and tell others about you?

These ideas may take time to implement, but you'll get there. Don't feel bad about starting with the basics and going from there. Soon enough you'll have a valuable marketing machine that boosts your business automatically.

Coming up, you'll have a great opportunity to test out your new measurement skills by learning about one of the most frequently screwed-up elements of a local company's marketing plan. By fixing what's likely to be broken here, you'll have a chance to see what a dramatic improvement looks like when you measure it.

⌘ ⌘ ⌘

Case Study: Measure What Matters

Small Business Owners are as pressed for time as anyone. But if you are going to successfully grow your business it takes a time investment and the discipline to put a system in place to ensure your marketing efforts produce results. Measurement and Analytics are a crucial part of this process.

Recently we completed a 6 month "guided coaching" program with 3 local small business owners representing diverse businesses – a residential and commercial cleaning company, a custom framing shop owner and an IT services provider. Over the course of this time together, and leveraging the Duct Tape Marketing System, these owners learned and implemented a focused approach to marketing that began with developing a marketing strategy and moved through creating, implementing and measuring the tactical plans that fuel their growth. Said one participant, "I no longer lose sleep worrying about how I'm going to market my business. I understand my target markets, value proposition and how to reach my target markets better than I ever have before."

One of the most valuable parts of this program is thinking through what to measure and analyze in their marketing efforts. Knowing the number of website visits, Facebook Likes and Twitter followers you have is great, but what really matters is how this engagement turns into lasting, profitable customer relationships. I coach my clients to start at the end – number of customers, profitability of customers, cost to acquire new customers, number of referring customers – and work backward from there to metrics like traffic and likes. Armed with the knowledge of the profitability of each type of customer relationship you can make very focused choices about the types and frequency of marketing programs you should run and their impact on your bottom line.

Mark Z. Fortune
www.fortunemarketinginc.com

⌘ ⌘ ⌘

Chapter Seven: Are Your Listings Helping or Hurting?

"To be trusted is a greater compliment than being loved."

George MacDonald

Many business owners are tempted to write off directory and reputation marketing as a last step in their marketing plan, the icing on the cake once they tackle all other marketing issues. They set up their online local business listings years ago, and called it a day. They count on their good names to protect them, or figure that since most of their customers are happy, that's good enough. Do what you do best, and word of mouth will follow.

Sorry to disappoint, but in this day and age, that's just not true anymore. Especially for local businesses trying to compete against bigger names, it's critical to take your online reputation seriously – in fact, it's one of the easiest ways to put your smaller business on equal footing with your bigger competitors.

And whether you know it or not, listings and directory companies have created content for your business. You are listed on their sites and these sites are gathering traffic to make recommendations or provide information on your business to local consumers. So, shouldn't you make sure it is the most compelling and accurate information available? Plus, a well-tended and differentiated strategy for reputation management and directory placement can be a significant competitive advantage as many, if not most, of your competitors are not doing this.

Nowadays you need to actively mold your online reputation, or you run the risk of letting others do it for you. Would you let some stranger behind the wheel of a car that had your business name and logo stamped all over it? No? We didn't think so. So don't leave your online reputation to chance, either. In so many ways your customers are more in charge of your business and reputation than ever before. And, the better they feel about their experience with you the more they will not only improve your reputation but will also refer you new business!

See, you don't only exist on your own website or social media platforms. Your name is bandied about in dozens of other places too. Anywhere a customer can leave a review about you, in fact, you run the risk of turning your reputation over to them. However, if you're vigilant and know how to manage your reputation and list your business in online search directories, you can ensure that you manage your good name.

In this chapter we're going to talk about how to manage your online reputation so that when customers search for you in the heavily trafficked and incredibly influential online sphere, they'll find good results, not lukewarm or bad ones. In addition to covering reputation marketing so you can protect your name, we'll take a look at directory marketing – which isn't nearly as scary as it sounds, so don't worry. These two marketing strategies will do wonders for protecting your online identity and preserving customer trust. And, proactive strategies in these areas will also allow you to avoid all of the telemarketing calls you are getting currently from sales reps wanting to manage your directory listings for you.

What's in a Name?

Simply put: everything.

Think about Enron. The name conjures up images of broken trust, greediness, bankrupt morals, ugly legal disputes, and hard falls. Now think about Apple. If you're like most, now you're getting images of excellence, innovation, horizon-breaking, customer service revolutionizing and a product line to make your mouth water. These two simple names, Apple versus Enron, epitomize the best and worst about business today. Which category would you prefer to be in?

Your reputation is everything, because your name will either tell customers they can trust you and should absolutely walk through your door and give you their business, or that they can't and should stay away at all costs. Social proof is powerful, too, so whatever the reviews say online will dictate how prospects treat you. Many people are slow to believe this is true, but according to a survey by Dimensional Research, a full 90 percent of people use online reviews to help them make a purchasing decision. In research conducted in 2014 by BrightLocal specifically about local small businesses, nearly 40% of people regularly read reviews before making a purchase decision and 85% of people read up to 10 reviews before buying!

(http://www.brightlocal.com/2014/07/01/local-consumer-review-survey-2014/#internet)

Unfortunately, it only takes one nasty review to turn potential customers away from you forever… especially if it's the only review out there.

Oddly enough, many marketing efforts take a backward approach by focusing solely on acquiring new customers versus ensuring great experiences and referrals from their existing customers. They launch a marketing campaign by putting lots of effort into drumming up business, using social media, email, mailers and more to send people to their various locations, both online and off.

While it feels great when your marketing efforts produce results, this isn't the only approach. Think about it: Someone gets excited to use your service, and hurries off to their computer, only to discover that you don't really have an online presence to speak of. Sure, you've got a site (doesn't everyone these days?), but you don't have any customer reviews, you're not listed in any directories, and they can't find anyone talking about you. Or worse, they are talking about you, and what they're saying is not good. The ability to use the great things your best customers think about you across online marketing channels can be your most powerful competitive differentiator.

Even if you have somewhere valuable to send people (like your website or your brick-and-mortar business) and do pretty good business, you are missing a golden opportunity if you just leave it at that. Because one of two things will eventually happen:

1. You forget to monitor your online reputation and a nasty review undoes all your hard marketing work.

Or…

2. Your potential customer searches for reviews on you, can't find any, and takes it as a bad sign, despite your good website and excellent marketing work.

With so much riding on other people's opinions, you've got to make sure those opinions showcase you in the best light. This means getting people talking about you in a good way.

Own Your Name in Search Results

If you want to keep your reputation intact, and hopefully awesome, then you need to know what people are saying about you.

Consider using a local online reputation monitoring service. These services allow you to search for your name, company name, URL and the main keywords used by or describing your business. It will let you know when your name pops up on social media, in forums, or elsewhere on the web. The good reviews can provide not only an emotional boost, but an excellent window into what you're doing right and should reinforce. The negative reviews, on the other hand, can point the way toward where you might do better.

They serve a more important purpose, however. Negative reviews point very clearly toward places where you need to spend more marketing time. Let's say you've used a local reputation monitoring service to discover that there's some nasty press about you on Twitter. Unfortunately, there's no way to remove that press, and thanks to recent changes in Google's algorithm, tweets are now easier than ever to find via search.

Don't panic, though. You can combat the negative reviews by bumping them down in search. How? By getting lots of positive tweets that mention your name. These are especially valuable when they come from others, so you might launch a marketing campaign to get your customers and clients to tweet about you, or establish partnerships with other businesses to exchange tweets that pump up your business names.

Or let's say you recently received a devastating review on Facebook. Rather than rolling over, let this be your motivation to fix any underlying problems that caused the bad review – and then get a lot of great reviews. There are lots of ways to go about this, including:

- Ask your customers to give you a review.
- Hand out explicit instructions detailing how to write a Facebook review.
- Review a partner company (since B2B reviews are totally valid).
- Put a Facebook badge on your website.
- Announce that customers can "Find Us on Facebook!" to encourage the likelihood of organic reviews.

Once you have twenty good reviews in the 4- or 5-star category, no one will mind that single bad review any longer. Boom. You've taken back your reputation and built up a valuable business asset at the same time. Not only that, you've buffered yourself against future negative reviews, because even if you get a few more, your good reviews will still outweigh them, especially if you keep your Facebook marketing engine running over time… and why wouldn't you, since it's already in place?

Keep in mind; the easiest way to avoid negative reviews is to deliver excellent customer experiences. And while there is no way to keep every customer delighted all of the time, your positive experiences will outweigh the negative ones, but you need a plan for maximizing the impact of positive reviews as you grow your business.

You Can Use SEO to Protect Yourself, Too

You really must own your name in the search results themselves. No matter how hard you work on Twitter and Yelp, a customer can still wreak havoc on your business by devoting a blog to ruining you or creating a forum dedicated to your demise. The answer for Google (or other search engines) is the same as for other online platforms: Push the bad review down with good content that will take its place. Plus, the more positive reviews you receive, the better your results in search pages look.

Work with partners to exchange good reviews on your blogs, for example, and devote some of your marketing efforts, such as press releases or landing pages to interviews from local media or bloggers. Build your online presence with videos, press releases, and an ever-expanding website, so more pages that you control pop up in search, pushing down the negative pages. Every page that talks about you in a good light combats the negativity and pushes it further down in rank, until eventually it's so far back it won't be noticed. To build a hedge of protection like this, you need a reputation marketing plan.

Report? Reuse? Repair?

You've probably been pitched by companies offering some form of reputation monitoring or marketing services. There are actually three levels of intensity here.

- Reputation monitoring is just keeping an eye on the online chatter and reporting what's being said about your company. You can't fix a problem if you don't know it exists.

- Reputation marketing includes monitoring, but goes one step further to help you get more positive reviews and use them to attract more new customers. Happy customers are coaxed into leaving glowing reviews; unhappy customers get heard and problems are fixed so that they become happy customers.

- Reputation repair isn't usually needed – unless you haven't been monitoring and marketing your online reputation. This is a level of service no business owner wants to need; it means something has gone seriously wrong enough that an unhappy customer is doing major damage to your online reputation.

Create Your Reputation Monitoring and Marketing Plan

The trick to turning these reputation marketing tactics into a reusable plan is to streamline them so you never have to wonder what step to take next. There's no way around it – this is a labor-intensive process that requires some more advanced tech skills if you want to do it on your own.

However, by creating a reputation monitoring and marketing system that works, you'll stay on top of negative reviews, act quickly to bury them with positive content, hold on to that golden reputation you need and deserve, and use it to attract more ideal customers.

For reputation monitoring, the first step is to create a list of keywords, both positive and negative, that you think your business might be associated with. Combine your business name with common trigger words to create keywords such as "Your Business Name scam." Vary the spellings of your business name, products and services to cover the gamut of search terms that might be used.

The next step is to create a Google Alerts system so you'll be notified of every online mention of your business. There are dashboard tools you can use to set up feeds so you can track the activity occurring on social media platforms, forums, blogs and search engines. While a comprehensive list of what you should follow is beyond the scope of this chapter, you should at least follow Twitter, Google and other search engines, and forums.

Now create feeds for all of your search terms on other major platforms. Simply search your individual keywords, and then add the page that pops up to a feed to add to your dashboard. Now you'll be alerted every time one of your keywords gets used across a range of platforms. Although it's a lot of work to get your feeds set up and monitor them, there are reputation-monitoring services you can use instead.

Reputation marketing takes reputation monitoring a step further, not only reporting what's being said, but also proactively seeking positive reviews. There are a lot of pitfalls you'll encounter if you try to do this on your own – so either learn exactly what you can and cannot do, or hire this complex task out to a specialist. For example, you've got to have a way to encourage happy customers to leave a positive review – and to encourage unhappy customers to let you know what happened and give you the chance to make things right. You can't pay or entice your customers to leave glowing reviews – and you can't gather them and post them yourself. The notable review sites have gotten extremely sophisticated over the past few years, and if you try to game them, you'll regret it.

The reward, whether you handle these tasks on your own or hire them out, is more than worth it: an up-to-the-minute picture of what others are saying about you online, allowing you to jump in and fix a damaged reputation before it even takes hold – plus the power to build and market your online reputation so that your hard-earned good name goes to work for you, building your credibility with new customers before they ever buy from you.

Boost Your Online Presence with Directory Listings

Directory listings are another great way to ensure that potential clients and customers know you exist, and find a ready-and-waiting online presence when they go to search for you. A well-rounded presence in directories can also help to ensure that negative reviews do less harm, since people will see a lot of positive reviews and neutral online presences combating them.

Because customers expect to work only with businesses that are established and well-respected, you should have a listing in most of the major directories if you want to ensure they take you seriously.

These include:
- Google+ and Google My Business
- Yelp
- Bing Places
- Yahoo! Local
- Yellow Pages
- Local Directories

In order to be listed in a directory, you need to be a brick-and-mortar business, but this generally isn't a problem for local businesses. Specifically, you need:

- A business name or DBA
- A local phone number that matches the city in which you operate
- A physical street address that isn't shared or a PO box
- Regular face-to-face contact with your customers at that address (to ensure you aren't a virtual business posing as a local one)

The topic of directory marketing could form an entire chapter (or book) in and of itself, but for now be aware that you should begin claiming your business listings across directory platforms and undergoing the verification process for each one. Make sure that the listing information you provide is exactly the same for each directory – if there are variations in spelling or your location's specifics, you'll defeat the purpose of submitting your business.

After you've claimed your listings, then you can move on to more advanced topics such as getting citations. These are mentions of your business name and address on other sites across the web that increase your credibility, and cleaning up old listings so that they aren't duplicated, don't contain incorrect content, and transition seamlessly with you through a physical move or other change. Not so hard, right? OK, yeah, maybe it is – but it needs to be done.

Once you master the concept of reputation and directory marketing, you can create a marketing plan that will help you stay on top of everything that gets said about you online. This will help you effectively combat negativity before it has a chance to take root and impact your business.

The bottom line is that you've got to provide an excellent customer experience. You'll get reviews whether you want them or not – reputation management is like an insurance policy to make sure your online reviews help and don't hurt you.

In the process of minding what's being said about you online, you'll build a shiny, 5-star reputation that you can use to attract more customers, partners and important relationships, all of which will propel your business to the next level, and you along with it.

Prospective customers really do their research before they do business with a company, and reviews play a huge part in forming their impression of your business before they make contact with you. However, while your reviews are enough to attract or repel some customers, others are going to do even more extensive research before they'll make your phone ring or your door swing. Next up, we're going to take a look at how you can get Google to send business your way.

Even though reputation monitoring and marketing and managing your directory listings are necessary pains in the neck, thank goodness not every marketing task feels as hard as doing brain surgery. The next one we're going to talk about is a lot more humane – and human-oriented. Ready?

⌘ ⌘ ⌘

Case Study: Online Reviews: 24/7 Word Of Mouth Advertising

We've been working with the leading plumbing & HVAC Company in Kansas City for several years. Bob Hamilton Plumbing + Heating + A/C + Rooter (www.bobhamilton.com) has been a marketing leader in our metro area for decades. Yet as strong and creative as they have been with traditional marketing, when they came to us five years ago, their web visibility was not nearly as strong as their offline presence. At first, we focused on organic search engine optimization and combined that with a proactive online reputation strategy. In a few short years, the company went from a few dozen reviews to several hundred – with nearly 300 on Google alone.

By focusing on SEO and reputation management, we stumbled on the Holy Grail of Internet marketing. People trust Google and they trust genuine customer reviews. When a company pops up first on Google showing many more positive reviews than their competitors, the phone starts ringing like never before.

All it takes is a clear strategy with the discipline to work reputation management into your company's daily routine. There are clear and ethical tactics and tools that enable you to prompt your customers to leave good reviews in the right places, while simultaneously catching bad reviews before they get posted online.

Check the resources web page to see how to take first steps towards implementing a killer online reputation strategy:
http://localleadgenbook.com/resources/

Phil Singleton
www.kcseopro.com

⌘ ⌘ ⌘

Chapter Eight: People Like Connecting with YOU

"Communication – the human connection – is the key to personal and career success."

Paul J. Meyer

For small business owners online marketing is a world full of opportunity and challenge. Online marketing can be extremely profitable and rewarding, but it can also be highly frustrating and confusing without a strong game plan. We've discussed websites, search marketing, and online advertising in other parts of this book. Now it's time to turn our attention to email marketing and social media.

Before you panic, know this: you are not alone in your anxiety about social media or your confusion about email marketing. To many of you, especially if you're older or threw your shingle up long before the advent of such marketing strategies, these can feel vaguely threatening or downright disingenuous. Before you judge, though, take a moment to think about your goal with any marketing endeavor. What it really comes down to is people, right?

Good news. Email marketing and social media are all about reaching people and expanding your audience of potential customers. Better news: by using these tactics, you can reach more of your ideal customers than you ever thought possible by spending far less than you would on traditional marketing activities. Let's consider first email marketing and then social media, focusing on how to get up and running with minimal time and effort.

Email Marketing: Big Bang for Your Buck

With email marketing, you can send a message to thousands of people for little or sometimes no money whatsoever. Right now, it's perhaps the most efficient and cost-effective way to communicate with large numbers of customers, clients and prospects.

Email marketing has several other advantages too. It allows you to partner up with other small businesses in your area, exchanging value and building relationships. Furthermore, it enables you to gather information on your ideal customer type, since the profiles of the people who have already subscribed align closely with the profiles of people you are still working to attract. By taking note of the links that get clicked, the emails that get opened and the calls to action that get met, you can learn tons about your customer base. You can then use these analytics to capture more customers and more market share. Email marketing is highly track-able, giving you quick insight to what works and what doesn't. It also is very quick to deploy – while it does require time to plan a strong campaign, the actual execution can occur very fast.

There are two primary challenges to email marketing – building a list and knowing what content to include in your email marketing campaign. In the next section we will address this in detail so that you won't get stuck for ideas when starting your email marketing campaign.

Before you begin marketing through email, there are two quick things you need to do. First, you need to establish an email address that ends in your domain, instead of one that is yourbusiness@gmail.com (or Hotmail, yahoo, etc.). The allure of using a "provider" email domain is that they're very easy to set up and they're free. The downside is that they give your target markets an unprofessional view of your business. Every domain provider and website hosting company includes email on your domain with your account

– use it! Does it look more professional to you to see an email from mycompany@gmail.com or to see one from "bob@mycompany.com"? The second is far more professional and indicates that you're in business to build relationships for the long run.

Second, you need to sign up with an email service provider (ESP) such as MailChimp, Aweber, Constant Contact, or Infusionsoft (there are many of these providers; these are the ones the authors use most). These are all easy to use and very affordable tools for email marketing that not only provide very creative templates for effective email marketing, but also manage your customer email information and subscriptions so you do not have to spend a lot of manual effort on anti-spam compliance.

Special Offer:

Visit localleadgenbook.com/resources to see a list of popular email service providers and sign up for a free trial.

Intent and Content Matters

It is important to think through what you want to do with email marketing and how you want to achieve that. Specific tactics for email marketing can include:

- Customer newsletters – stay in touch, promote new products, and make special offers.
- Promotional or seasonal email – promoting specific offerings or new products.
- Transactional email – even basic emails like shipping notifications, or sending invoices should be used to reinforce engagement with your business.
- Autoresponders – these are a series of emails that are simple to set up and provide an automated method for you to stay in touch with your customers and prospects. For example an email that is automatically sent thanking a new sign-up for your email newsletter that is followed three days later with an offer to download other content, or to sign up for a product demo, or a promotional offer on a first purchase, etc.

Most email marketing focuses on the regularly delivered customer newsletter, so let's spend some time discussing this kind of touch. Launching a regular email newsletter isn't second nature to most. Start small, by deciding how often you'll send your newsletter. Weekly is best, but at least monthly is a must. Any less frequently than that and people may begin to forget who you are, at which point you risk losing them.

Then create a template for your email newsletters. Once you're experienced, feel free to vary your template, but start with the following:

- A personalized greeting ("Hi Mark" instead of "Hi All"), which any decent email marketing service will allow you to do
- A two- or three-sentence intro from the business owner about something exciting in the business, or a teaser for another section of the newsletter
- Your educational content: a tip, an article, a blog post (either the whole thing, if it's short, or a paragraph with an outside link if it's longer)
- SEC, or Someone Else's Content, well attributed to avoid plagiarism and from a well-known expert in the business. This could be a strategic partner's blog post, video, or content from a well-respected industry resource
- Featured partner section, if you have someone whose niche audience is similar to yours and with whom you like exchanging referrals
- Featured customer with a testimonial
- Call to action, where you actually sell to your customers, taking up no more than 20 percent of your newsletter
- Signoff

Let's take a minute to talk about the featured partner. This is a great opportunity to add value to a relationship, especially if featured partners don't have a list of their own. You can either rotate through a regular cast, or just target the same strategic partner in every newsletter. Invite them to create some content to insert into the newsletter to showcase their experience and add value to your email marketing.

The featured customer section allows you to showcase how well your products or services work for real people. Keep in mind that you can't use customer names without consent, but many people are happy to help if you ask. Your customers may be so pleased to be featured that they'll share your newsletter with others... voila, more free marketing. Where possible, include photos with testimonials to make it more realistic.

Stay On the Right Side of the Law

Before you get excited and just start emailing people, though, keep compliance in mind. The CAN-SPAM act dictates how and under what circumstances you may send commercial emails to someone:

1. Your header information, including "To," "From," and routing information, must be true, so do not falsify or fudge it.
2. Your subject line must truly reflect the nature of the email.
3. You must acknowledge that the email is an ad, rather than trying to sneak into someone's inbox posing as a friend, etc.
4. You must include a physical mailing address registered with the USPS.
5. Clear opt-out options must be included in every email (email marketing services do this for you).
6. You must honor all opt-out requests immediately.
7. Any email that goes out under your name is your responsibility even if you've outsourced the job to others, so monitor employees or service providers closely.

If you're new to email marketing, the main facts you should keep in mind are a) you must give the recipient a way to opt out of your newsletter, and b) you must have a physical address associated with it. That's just one reason that sending a marketing message from a regular email account (not managed by an ESP) is a very bad idea. Chances are you haven't inserted your address in the signature line, and all opt-out requests will need to be handled manually, whereas an ESP like Constant Contact, MailChimp, or

Aweber includes an opt-out link at the bottom of every newsletter. Do yourself a favor and use one of these reputable email marketing services so you don't have to worry about this at all.

(Need more info? Download the CAN-SPAM Act Compliance Guide published by the FTC at www.ftc.gov)

Building Your List: Encouraging Email Signups

So you know the rules, you've got an email marketing service and a pretty good template, you want to get started… but you have no one to email to. That's okay: it's where most people start.

Now it's time to get people to sign up for your list. And your list is gold – this is not a trivial step! Building a high-performing list of opt-in email subscribers is arguably one of the most powerful marketing tactics you can use. Many small business owners put a subscription box on their websites to the effect of "Sign up for our email newsletter". This may work for a well-known brand that has loyal followers, but for most local business owners, the last thing that people want to do is sign up for your email newsletter.

You've got to give people something in return for getting their email address and permission to market to them. If someone signs up, you'll give them an eBook you wrote, a checklist, a coupon or some other type of "free gift" that will make their lives easier, save them money, entertain, etc. The offer needs to provide value while moving you closer to you goal of acquiring customers and building relationships.

Although this works very well, beware: if your free gift and the content of your newsletters aren't closely aligned, you'll probably lose subscribers. You shouldn't simply offer people the chance to win a free iPad by signing up for your email list and then expect people to stay invested through weekly emails about plumbing and plumbing services. Instead, if you're a plumber, you might give out a downloadable PDF entitled "Time for New Pipes? Take Our Quiz and Find Out." It's useful, it could save consumers money, it makes them want to know what else you've got to say, and it could even encourage them to become your customer in the long run. The "free iPad" offer just encourages people to sign up (often with fake email addresses) who have no genuine interest in your business. Tie your offers to your business.

Some final words on email marketing – be realistic about the results your email efforts return in terms of open rates, click-throughs and conversions. As you can see here: http://mailchimp.com/resources/research/email-marketing-benchmarks/ email open and click rates vary wildly by industry. And you'll see that a 50% open rate is a very high, industry-leading result. So, build a permission-based list, provide compelling content and you should have no trouble topping these averages.

Social Media Marketing: Don't Create a Social Media Ghost Town

The topic of social media marketing could fill several small books, but if you're a novice, you should start with a brief overview to avoid overwhelm. Despite great intentions, newbies often allow overwhelm to ruin their social media efforts, often doing more harm than good.

How? Let's call it the Social Media Ghost Town Effect. It goes a little something like this: You hear that everyone's on Twitter, so you figure you need to be as well. You jump on, spending the better part of a day creating an account, choosing a profile picture, creating the perfect tagline and adding followers. You post like a champ for a few weeks. Nothing much happens. Your attention is drawn elsewhere. You forget about Twitter entirely. Before you know it, a few months or years have gone by and the last thing on your Twitter account is a cheerful "Happy Thanksgiving 2012!"

This is more than a bad social media strategy; it can be downright damaging to your business. When people search for your business social media profiles will often turn up in the search results. If no posts have been made to those accounts in several months or years, people immediately start asking questions. Where are they? Are they still in business? Do they have nothing to say? As you can see, none of these questions are good, so you don't want to give potential customers or clients a chance to ask them.

Instead of launching a full-scale frontal assault on every social media platform, choose one or two and stick with it for a bit. Post daily, or weekly at a minimum. Play to your strengths so that you don't get burned out. Respond to customers and prospects when they engage you through social media. During this time, refuse to get distracted by the newest social media players; this landscape changes constantly. If you can't commit to such a strategy yourself, hire someone else to do it for you. Just be sure they know what they're talking about, or you risk ruining your reputation all over again.

What Should You Share?

In order to post good content that builds your business instead of wastes your time, money and energy, you need a plan for what you're trying to accomplish. Just rehashing what your business does, continuously sharing other people's content, or operating as a lookalike social media channel based on one of your competitors isn't going to bring in business. You need a clear direction for what you're posting and why.

This not only varies by business, it varies by platform. Twitter is a medium that encourages brevity, only giving you 140 characters with which to work. So what you say on Twitter will be short, pithy and to the point. On Facebook, however, people will take the time to read 100 words or so, so you can insert an opinion, flesh out a sale or other opportunity, or give a solid tip to save customers time or money. Google+ allows for even longer content, while Pinterest is image-based and people will barely read anything that accompanies the picture. On the other hand, LinkedIn is all about relationships and networking, and people get really turned off by salesy approaches.

You also have many options when it comes to what type of content you will post. Here are a few examples:

- Your own content – amplify what you have created on your website
- Someone else's content
- Videos or images
- Information about area activities, organizations, schools, etc.
- Quotes
- Discounts, coupons or sales

There are many ways to use social media, including:

- Building relationships
- Instilling trust
- Proving expertise
- Featuring products
- Providing customer service (answering questions)
- Holding contests

Of course, there are many other ways to use it as well; these are just a few of the most common. Be clear on what your goals are before you launch a social media endeavor, because your actions will change accordingly.

Perhaps an example will help. Let's say you want to focus on building a Facebook page that will encourage people to sign up for your mailing list or use your products and services. For this type of endeavor, you can share all types of content, which you create and which you borrow from others.

You can also feature coupons and deals that will encourage them to come to you for appointments or to buy products. And you can subtly hint that the deals and content are even BETTER if people sign up for your newsletter. You can then link to the newsletter signup page, where people can opt in to your list and receive their free gift. In this way, you use social media to promote your brand and business at the same time that you grow your list.

For example, if you are an HVAC contractor your Facebook page can highlight the seasonal maintenance services you provide, linking back to your website asking for email newsletter signups in return for a download of your "10 Tips to Keeping Your Systems Running" eBook. Facebook also is a great medium for sharing photos of you delighting your customers and encouraging them to endorse and review your company.

As this example highlights, eventually your email marketing and social media efforts will become intertwined and streamlined, allowing you to maximize the return for your efforts. Though the learning curve is steep, the payoff is more than worth it.

Facebook is also evolving as an effective advertising medium, enabling you to create highly targeted ads on their platform that can deliver your offers to the right audience at the right time. With Facebook advertising, you can target people based on age, interests, profession, income level, and a host of other demographics. You can use the ads to drive traffic to a website, generate "likes" for a Facebook page, or promote a special offer for your business. Visit localleadgenbook.com/resources for more information about Facebook advertising options.

Email marketing and social media marketing are, at their core, all about connecting with your customers and prospects in a way that makes them want even more from you. They know you; they like you; they trust you so much that your business becomes the only one – or the most important one – that comes to mind when they think about the products and services you sell. That sort of mindshare is the hallmark of truly successful marketing, and shows that you've won the hearts and minds of your ideal customers.

These tactics accomplish winning favor with your target market using technology, but next up we'll talk about building an entire team of people who will work hard to spread your message to every prospective customer they meet.

⌘ ⌘ ⌘

Case Study: Bar & Restaurant Quickly and Affordably Grows Its Followers

A local bar that we were working with wanted to attract more young professionals and recent college grads. Since this demographic group uses Facebook on a regular basis, we decided to try a Facebook advertising campaign targeting these types of customers. Thanks to Facebook's very detailed options for ad targeting based on a variety of demographics—including age, education level, income, and geographic location—this was very easy to do.

Instead of immediately trying to get people to click through to the bar's website, at first all we did was use the ads to generate "likes" for the bar's Facebook page. We spent $5 per day (about $150 per month) until the page had a decent number of "likes".

At that point, we added a second ad campaign that "boosted" posts from the bar's blog to the news feeds of people who had "liked" the page, as well as their friends. The posts we selected to boost referenced specials and events being held at the bar. We budgeted about $80 a month for this second part of the campaign. This formula added 5,000 new followers to the bar's Facebook page in just 10 months, and it has been picking up steam ever since.

Justin Sturges

www.systemadik.com

⌘ ⌘ ⌘

Chapter Nine: Energizing Your Unpaid Salesforce (Your Customers)

"Referrals aren't given easily. If you don't take the time to establish credibility, you're not going to get the referral. People have to get to know you. They have to feel comfortable with who you are and what you do."

Dr. Ivan Misner
Founder of BNI

Ever stayed at a Double Tree hotel? If so, you know exactly what delighted customers look like. They're easy to spot – they're wiping the remnants of a gooey, warm chocolate chip cookie off of their lips. Where at many hotels you count yourself lucky to get a copy of the USA Today and leave without taking bedbugs home with you, this place gives you a fresh, warm cookie when you check in.

One way you, as a comparatively small local business, can out-gun your bigger competitors is by taking customer delight to a whole new level. In fact, when you master the art of customer delight, you'll find that other businesses practically line up to hand new customers, THEIR customers, to you.

Customer delight is at the heart of referral marketing. When other business owners see that just about every customer who walks through your door turns into a raving fan, they want you on their team. They'll send their best customers to you (assuming you're not direct competitors, of course!) because they trust you'll take great care of them, simultaneously making them look like problem-solving geniuses.

So, you're probably thinking, "That's great, but how do I turn every customer into a raving fan? And where can I find other business owners who will send their customers to me?" Funny you should ask, because that's exactly what we're going to talk about for the rest of this chapter.

Nobody Talks About Boring Businesses

Let's address the issue of turning every customer into a raving fan first. The best way to do this is to do something unexpected to surprise and delight those who do business with you—the way that Double Tree Hotels does with their warm chocolate chip cookies. You see, delivering quality customer service isn't something that sets you apart—that's just doing what's expected of you. There isn't anything exciting about having your CPA file your tax return on time, or having your local auto repair shop check your windshield wiper fluid during a full-service oil change. So, how can you go from routine to exciting? Let's take a look at how one local business owner did just that, and maybe you'll get some inspiration.

Justin Hankins is a Virginia Beach-based wedding photographer who travels around the world documenting the happiest moments in people's lives (www.justinhankins.com). His customer service and photography skills are both outstanding, but several years ago he still needed something more to help set him apart from other great photographers and get people talking about his business. At that time, like just about every other photographer Justin delivered pictures to his clients in digital form on a DVD. This was around the time that iPads had recently been released and were still considered a "hot" electronic gadget, so Justin started delivering digital pictures to his clients on an iPad in addition to a DVD. The clients got to keep the iPad, and he even let them pick out what color iPad they wanted (the cost of the iPad was built into his photography fee). Doing this helped make his business a little more exciting, and generated more word of mouth referrals.

Are you starting to get the picture (pun intended)? Whether it's warm cookies or iPads, find a way to give your customers something they don't expect. Make it something unusual enough that the next time they're talking to a friend, they'll mention it—and recommend your business at the same time.

Making Referral Marketing Your SOP

If you think back to how you started your business, it was probably a whole lot of word of mouth. That's how it is for most businesses, actually. People you knew connected you with people they knew because they wanted to help you get started – and wanted you to help their friends at the same time. They knew you, liked you, and trusted you enough to send people your way.

That's essentially how referral marketing works. Of course, waiting for people to send business your way (or begging them to do so) isn't exactly a sound marketing tactic.

There's got to be a way to build a system to make sure it happens regularly.

You can create a standard operating procedure in your business to create a steady stream of new customers coming in, courtesy of other business owners who serve a target market that includes your ideal customers. Once you have a crystal clear picture of your ideal customer, think about what other businesses this ideal customer is likely to do business with – before, during, or after doing business with you.

Forge a connection with people in those related businesses and have a conversation about what it would be like to send referrals to one another. The more in-depth you can get in this discussion over time, the more likely you are to develop a highly-profitable and satisfying referral relationship. You want to dig deep to learn what a good referral looks like to both of you, what expectations (if any) come with sharing referrals, how you'll take care of referrals sent your way, and even what you'll do if something goes wrong along the way.

Building referral partnerships with other businesses takes time. You've got to connect at a level that builds trust – after all, you're contemplating trusting some of your precious customers in the hands of another business owner. You have to know they'll be taken care of with the same level of care that you give – that every experience will be the equivalent of a warm, gooey cookie.

Referral Marketing with BNI (Business Network International)

If you use it correctly, BNI can produce shockingly good results for your local service-based business. It doesn't matter what niche you're in – it can work. They say that BNI "works for every business, but not every person." There's a reason for that somewhat cryptic quote – BNI requires a significant time commitment (as well as a small financial commitment) for it to work for you.

What Is BNI?

BNI is the world's leading organization for networking and business referrals. It was started in 1985 by Dr. Ivan Misner, and currently has over 179,000 members representing every populated continent on the planet. There are over 7,000 BNI chapters, and all together those chapters generated over $8.5 billion worth of business for their members last year. That's an average of $1.2 million per chapter, which usually range in size from between 15–50 members. In other words, on average a BNI membership is worth roughly $47,000 in new revenue per year as a direct result of your membership. With an annual membership costing less than $600 (in the U.S.), that's about the best return on investment you can get when it comes to marketing your business.

How Does BNI Work?

BNI is organized into chapters, each serving a small geographic area. In large metro areas, you'll probably find several chapters; in small towns and rural areas, you might have to travel a bit to find a chapter. Each chapter allows only one of any particular business to join: one dentist, one lawn care business, one commercial printer, one car insurance broker, one life insurance broker; you get the idea. This rule protects you from your competitors hearing more about your marketing plans than you'd like – and keeps the referral process simple.

You'll meet each week for about ninety minutes – often for breakfast. You can't miss meetings without sending a substitute to represent you. The reason for such a rigid attendance policy is that regular attendance and close interaction is the best way for the group's members to get to know each other and stay top-of-mind so they can send referrals to one another.

The meetings are pretty structured, with an agenda that's designed to make sure everyone has a turn to speak, and that the environment feels safe and encouraging. This is great because you'll never have to fight to get attention at a BNI meeting – everyone gets a turn.

There are set times for:

- Open Networking – welcoming visitors, catching up with members, and discussing referrals
- Introductory Remarks – housekeeping details and welcoming visitors and guests
- Educational Moment – the group's educational coordinator will share a tip for better networking
- Business Card Exchange – they'll pass the stack of cards so everyone can replenish their stash and make it easy to refer one another
- Weekly presentations – the group's members get one minute each to talk about their business and say what sort of referrals they're looking for that week.
- Showcase Presentation – one member per meeting will give a 10-minute presentation to help the other members understand their business better.
- Referrals – each member presents the referrals they've gathered in the past week for other members of the group; also they'll give testimonials about any members they did business with recently.
- Conclusion – any general news and updates about the chapter.

You'll be in and out in ninety minutes – unless you decide to stay after to keep networking.

If you're interested in joining BNI, visit a chapter near you (preferably one with an opening for someone in your business niche) so you can experience it for yourself (go to BNI.com to search for your local chapter). Be sure to ask other members how BNI has worked for them. You may be astounded to hear about their excellent results.

If you do join BNI, there's a lot you can do to maximize your results. Here are some tips:

Participate

A core principle of BNI is participation. In order to get the best results, you need to show up to the weekly meetings, and meet one-to-one with other members outside of the weekly meetings to discuss how you can help each other reach your goals.

Use the Resources Provided

In BNI, there is a system and a process for everything. These systems have been developed based on over 30 years of experience helping small business owners improve their networking skills. Don't try to re-invent the wheel—just follow the system.

Be Patient

Don't expect your business to double the first month after joining BNI. There's a reason that the minimum membership term is a year—it make take months before you start seeing results. Give the members of your chapter time to get to know and trust you—and make the effort to get to know and trust them as well. In time, your efforts will be rewarded.

Although BNI may be the largest and best-known business networking organization, it certainly isn't the only one. Local Chambers of Commerce are a great place to find networking and strategic partnership opportunities, and they will probably be a good source of information about other networking or referral groups in your area. You can also check Meetup.com to see if there are any business-related groups operating near you. If for whatever reason BNI isn't a good fit for you, or if there isn't a nearby chapter with an opening in your niche, don't give up—investigate other opportunities to find like-minded business owners who might make good strategic partners.

Special Offer:

Want more tips about referral marketing? Check out *Renewable Referrals,* a book all about how to form long-lasting strategic partnerships with other business owners by one of the authors of this book.
Visit
www.LocalLeadGenBook.com/resources for details.

All in all, referral marketing can be one of the lowest-tech, highest-yield marketing tactics you ever use in your business. It capitalizes on your excellent reputation for customer care, leverages the power of your network, and cuts the sales cycle down to size because your new customers come to you already knowing, liking, and trusting you – because they know, like, and trust the person who sent them your way. The more you make doing business with you the equivalent of that warm, gooey cookie, the more you'll become known for delighting customers – and the more customers other businesses will send your way.

Referral marketing is one of the oldest marketing tactics out there – but it's one a shockingly high number of businesses forget to do. Next up, we're going to talk about another oldie but goodie that's come back into favor in light of the rise of the Internet.

⌘ ⌘ ⌘

Referral Marketing: Joining Forces to Serve More Clients Together

Whenever you can get new business referred to you, you've got a huge head start on closing the sale, because referral marketing and word-of-mouth marketing are some of the strongest forms of marketing and lead generation there is.

Anytime two businesses have the same customer base, but do not have products and services that compete against each other, a referral program could work well for everyone involved. Customers of Company A win because they hear about Company B in the normal course of business, then benefit by finding the top-notch products and services they want and need – often accompanied by an attractive discount. Companies A and B win because they get more ideal customers, and in some cases, even a financial reward for making the referral.

Quite simply, referral marketing allows you to leverage the trustworthy reputation of other businesses so that you both can serve more customers together than you could on your own.

As one of the co-authors of the book Renewable Referrals, I've had the opportunity to help many of my clients create referral partner programs that have yielded extremely positive results. Typically, we identify potential referral partners that make sense for our clients, then create and promote a referral program that creates a win for everyone involved. The next step is welcoming and educating our clients' referral partners so they're likely to use the program. We also list them on our clients' websites to maximize exposure for everyone. After launching the program, we promote and grow it to yield as many leads as our client wants.

Ray L. Perry
www.RayLPerry.com
www.MarketBlazer.com
www.NeedMarketing.com

Receive a free copy of Ray's book *Renewable Referrals*.
Visit www.raylperry.com/business-marketing-audit
for details.

⌘ ⌘ ⌘

Chapter Ten: The Hottest Old Tactic to Get New Business

> *"And none will hear the postman's knock*
> *Without a quickening of the heart.*
> *For who can bear to feel himself forgotten?"*

W.H. Auden

As a small business owner, it probably feels like you've already considered every marketing strategy and attention-getting program known to man for reaching out to new and existing customers. You've probably discarded a number of them for some very good reasons. Among them: too expensive, too complex, too time consuming, or too unfocused... and just too much of a handful for a small business owner who already has both hands full.

But did you know there's a proven, time honored marketing program that's simple to implement, relatively inexpensive, and consistently gets results? It's direct mail. We're going to take a look at direct mail in general, and also a few specific direct mail tools that you might want to add to your toolbox.

You might be surprised to hear us recommending a tactic this low-tech, but as old school as it might sound, it can be really effective if you do it right. As people's online inboxes fill to overflowing, it's now nearly a novelty for them to receive mail in their physical mailboxes. Rather than getting lost in a pile of paper, it's possible your direct mail piece will be just one of a very small stack they'll rifle through – and that makes it easier than ever to grab their attention.

Direct mail is a marketing program that mails out, usually via the US Postal Service, printed promotional material to a company's target audience. The printed material can be almost anything, from flat postcards to thick catalogs, but the goal is the same – to generate sales of the company's products or services. The audience can either be existing customers of the company, prospective customers, or strategic partners.

Direct mail advertising has been around for many decades, dating back to the Sears and Montgomery Ward catalogs of the 1800's, but it's still one of the most effective and profitable ways to attract new customers, or get existing customers to take buying action.

What Makes Direct Mail Effective?

So what's the big draw with direct mail? Why is it still considered one of the best ways to reach out to new and existing customers? First of all, unlike with email marketing, there aren't any government regulations concerning direct mail that you need to comply with. You also don't have to worry about SPAM filters blocking your direct mail pieces, as sometimes happens with email messages.

In addition, as you will shortly see, direct mail is very versatile – it can take many different forms such as letters, postcards, or packages.

Finally, direct mail is highly targetable. In fact, the most recent tools developed for direct mail allow you to very precisely control who will receive your message, and when. This is especially important for local and regional businesses that would like to do targeted, geographically specific mailings. You can set your target as specific as individual communities, and even neighborhoods within communities.

Since most local businesses sell their products and services within tightly targeted geographic areas, they don't necessarily need the wide-blast approach provided by newspaper, TV, radio, or other conventional forms of advertising. For example, at a very low cost a local car detailing business can focus on one small upscale neighborhood filled with luxury cars. They don't spend much money, yet they hit exactly the market they're after with no unwanted and money-wasting overlap.

Types of Direct Mail

As we just mentioned, one of the key advantages to direct mail is all the different forms it can take. Let's take a look at some of the most common forms of direct mail, along with their advantages and disadvantages.

Letters

Letters are one of the oldest forms of communication on the planet – heck, many of the books in the New Testament of the Bible are actually just early examples of direct mail letters! They work just as well today as they did back then, and they're the easiest form of direct mail to create. Just open up a business letter template in your favorite word processor program, type up your message, and print it out on your company letterhead.

The downside to letters, of course, is that they need to go in an envelope, which means that you'll need a first class postage stamp. It also means that someone needs to stuff and seal the envelopes. Finally, it means that there's a chance people won't even open the envelope and read your letter before tossing it in the trash. One way around this is to hand-write the address on the envelope instead of using a mailing label or printing it directly on the envelope – most people won't toss an envelope with a hand-written address before opening it.

In general, letters tend to work best for mailings to your existing customers and for B2B (business to business) direct mail campaigns.

Flyers, Brochures, and Booklets

Yes, you can send flyers, brochures, and booklets through the mail without putting them in an envelope – just make sure to follow USPS guidelines when creating your mail piece. These formats allow you to communicate more information than a simple letter, and also are more visually appealing. In addition, unlike letters, people won't need to open an envelope – meaning that they'll at least get a look at your message before tossing it.

The downside to flyers, brochures, and booklets is that in order to make them look professional, you'll probably need to get a graphic designer involved, thus adding to the expense of creating them. Also, in the case of booklets, postage will be a little higher.

Postcards

Postcards make great direct mail pieces for several reasons. Not only is postage cheaper (in the case of a standard size postcard), but thanks to online services like Vistaprint's postcard mailing service, you can have your postcards printed and sent out to your list without ever having to touch them. Also, as with flyers and brochures, there is no envelope for people to open.

The downside with postcards is that you have very limited space to work with, so they work best to communicate simple and clear calls to action that direct people to a website where they can learn more. You'll want to work with a graphic designer to make sure the front of your postcard is visually appealing and represents your brand well.

Lumpy Mail

"Lumpy mail" is an actual term used in the marketing industry to describe unusual mail pieces that grab your attention. The only limits to what you can do with lumpy mail are your postage budget and your own creativity. Some examples include:

- Bank bags with shredded dollars inside
- Trash can with your message crumpled up inside. Trash can says, "Before you throw this in the trash…"

- Prescription bottles with your message inside.
- Poker chips with your logo printed on them inside an envelope with your letter
- DVD mailers

There's even a website devoted to these types of mailings: 3Dmailresults.com. Depending on what you're mailing out, lumpy mail can get expensive, but the upside is that people are much more likely to open it and pay attention to your message. If done correctly, response rates for lumpy mail can be much higher than other forms of direct mail.

As you can see, there are quite a few different directions you can go with direct mail. Now let's take a look at some best practices when it comes to actually creating your mail piece.

Designing Your Mailing

The mailing you send out is a critical ingredient of your marketing strategy, and your opportunity to get your target audience to hear you out and see what you have to offer. This means that the design of your direct mail piece can be a deal breaker for your entire direct mail program if it's not done correctly.

First you should ask yourself a few questions about what you are trying to accomplish:

- What is the primary purpose of the piece (direct sales, lead capture, etc.)?
- Who is the target audience for the mailing (current customers, prospective customers, possible strategic partners, etc.)?
- What are the primary benefits I can offer?
- What call to action should I have in the piece?
- How do I want my business to be reflected by the piece?

Once you have the answers to these questions, the design step will flow much more smoothly.

Design Components

Here are a few things that are essential components of a direct mail piece:

Headline – The headline is the most important part of your message. When it's good it can grab the reader's attention. When it's bad, it turns the reader off to the entire piece. Try to use short, direct headlines that don't sound like a sales pitch. They should encourage the reader to delve further into the piece instead of throwing it away. For example, if a local auto repair shop was using a sweepstakes to capture names and email addresses of prospective customers, they might send out a postcard with the headline "Enter to Win Free Oil Changes for Life".

Copy – Copy is critical. Start off with your value proposition, but make sure it's brief and to the point. Remember, you have a very short amount of time to get the prospect to take action. Use facts and concise statements, and even bullet points to make the text stand out. Don't try to explain all the details of an offer. Simply tease the prospect enough to make them want to learn more. Naturally, correct grammar and spelling is critical.

Call to Action – This is almost as important, or even as important, as the headline. You need to have a clear call to action that tells the reader exactly what you want them to do, and how you want them to do it. In the case of the auto repair shop sweepstakes, the call to action might be "Visit www.MyAutoShop.com/sweepstakes or call xxx-xxxx to enter!"

Signature – This section may take the form of an actual signature, as in the case of a direct mail letter, or it could simply be your logo and contact information. Triple-check your contact information to make sure it's correct—one wrong digit in your phone number could ruin your entire mailing!

Presentation

After you've crafted the message for your direct mail piece, have a graphic artist turn the message into a visually appealing design that professionally represents your brand (make sure your designer is familiar with USPS guidelines regarding placement of text and graphics on your chosen type of mail piece). In the case of a direct mail letter, make sure you use professionally designed letterhead branded with your logo and colors. For flyers and postcards, don't use too many graphics or images. Both are good, but trying to put too much into a small area will be too much to look at and ultimately unattractive – meaning it will get tossed.

Another mistake to avoid is font overuse. This is not the same as too much text. If your font is too small it will be hard to read, but if too big it can be overwhelming to the reader. If it's a combination of different fonts it will seem unprofessional. Remember, the mail piece might be the very first impression someone has of your business. If it looks it was designed by a third grade art student, what message does that send about your company?

Creating Your Mailing List

Now that you have your mail piece ready, it's time to put together your mailing list. If you're doing a mailing targeting your current customers, then this part should be easy – you can simply export your customer's information from your bookkeeping or Customer Relationship Management (CRM) software (you do have the mailing address of all your customers, right?).

If you are targeting people who are NOT your customers, you have a couple of options for creating your mailing list. You can simply purchase one from a marketing service like InfoUSA , which allows you to buy lists of consumers or businesses based on just about any criteria you can imagine. If you don't have the money to purchase a list, you can assemble one yourself from publicly available databases and records, but this can be extremely time-consuming.

Another option would be to get a mailing list from a strategic partner or organization that you belong to. For example, if you're targeting businesses, the local chamber of commerce might provide you with their mailing list – if you're a member, of course. If none of the above options makes sense for you, there's actually a service provided by the USPS that allows you to do direct mailings without even having a list – more on that in a minute.

Regardless of how you get your list, you want to make sure that it's as targeted as possible. Simply putting more people on your list for the sake of having a larger list won't improve your results – it will just waste your money. Now might be a good time to review the ideal customer description you created after reading chapter one and make sure the people or businesses on your list match that description.

Once you've got your list ready, it's finally time to send your mail piece. You can do this yourself, have your staff to it, or hire a virtual assistant to do it for you. In some cases you can use an online service that both prints and sends your mail piece – for example, Vistaprint's postcard mailing service. The truth is there are many services and tools to help you with your direct mail campaigns, and we couldn't possibly list them all here. However, there are two services that are so helpful and unique that we feel a chapter on direct mail just wouldn't be complete without mentioning them: EDDM, and Send Out Cards.

EDDM

EDDM, which stands for "Every Door Direct Mail", is a relatively new tool created by the US Postal Service that has dramatically changed how the direct mail game is played.

Simply put, EDDM is a cost-effective and easy way to reach current and prospective customers within your geographic area of business without having to buy or create a mailing list and keep it up to date. You're essentially getting your mailing list from the keeper of the mailing list – the post office!

You simply create a mail piece that meets the specific guidelines published by the USPS for the program, select the postal routes that most closely match your target audience using the tool on the EDDM website, place your order online, and then take your mail piece to your local post office. From there it gets delivered to each household or business on your selected postal routes (yes, you can even decide if you want to only target residential or commercial addresses on a given postal route).

The US Postal Service has two different kinds of EDDM programs, depending on the size of your company. There is the EDDM program designed for larger businesses sending out tens of thousands or even hundreds of thousands of pieces per day. The other is for smaller, more localized businesses. The biggest difference between the two programs has to do with Post Office requirements.

The larger mailing program – mailing over 5000 pieces per day – requires a mail permit. The smaller more localized program does not. This program falls under the USPS Every Door Direct Mail – Retail Plan.

The EDDM retail plan allows you to target very specific areas at an extremely low rate, but there is no need to get a mail permit. The nice thing about this program is its ease of implementation, since you don't need to know addressee or street names of target customers. You simply need to know the general geographic areas to target and the program will take care of the rest.

EDDM is a great program for businesses whose ideal customers tend to be clustered together in well-defined geographic areas. Examples would include lawn care and other home improvement companies, auto repair shops, restaurants, certain types of professional practitioners, or unisex hair salons. It would not be a good program for businesses that define their ideal customers based primarily on demographics not closely related to geographic location – for example, bridal shops. Those types of businesses might benefit more from the next tool on our list.

Send Out Cards

Send Out Cards is unlike most direct mail services in that its intended use is not to send out hundreds or thousands of mail pieces at once. Instead, it's designed to help you send highly personal messages and gifts one at a time as a way of keeping in touch with customers and prospects. For example, if you know your customers' birthdays, you can have the service automatically send them each a card on their individual birthdays, addressed to them personally, and using their name in the message inside the card. You can even have the message written in your handwriting – all without you lifting a finger! Here's how it works:

- First, create a Send Out Cards account and upload your list of contacts to your account.

- Next, use the online editor to design your mail piece. You can send either postcards or several different styles of folding cards, and customize them however you want with your company branding.

- If you want, you can upload a sample of your handwriting and have the service create a font based on your handwriting, or you can use the fonts provided.

- Decide who you want to send your mail piece to, and when you want to send it. The service will automatically insert the person's name in the appropriate places on the card.

- Decide if you want to send a gift with the card. Choose from dozens of available gifts such as brownies, pens, or even audio books.

- The card (and gift, if selected) will be sent by the service at the appropriate time.

Not only can you use the service to send one-time cards or gifts, you can also create direct mail drip campaigns that send a series of cards over a period of time. This is ideal for businesses that have a long-term relationship with their customers (which, hopefully, is most of you). For example, you can add a new customer to a campaign that immediately sends them a thank-you card, and then sends them a postcard featuring a different coupon once every month or two for the next year. After adding them to the campaign, all the cards will get sent automatically at the appropriate time with no additional action required on your part.

Special Offer:
If you'd like to give Send Out Cards a try, visit localleadgenbook.com/resources to sign up for a free trial.

Be Patient

We would be remiss if we didn't end our chapter on direct mail by setting some realistic expectations for the results you're likely to get from your mailing. In most cases, response rates from a highly targeted and well-done direct mail campaign will be somewhere between 1-3%. You may have to send multiple mailings to the same list to get those results—in fact, conventional wisdom recommends sending at least five mailings to the same list.

At first, a response rate of 1-3% may not seem very good. However, consider the fact that for most local businesses, the lifetime value of a customer is quite high – sometimes thousands or even tens of thousands of dollars. Including printing and postage, it would only cost roughly $300 to send five postcard mailings to a list of 100 people. A 3% response rate from that campaign would be three new customers for the business in question. For most businesses, that's an excellent return on investment, but if that's not the case for you, you're probably better off trying a different marketing tactic. In fact, you might want to try the tactic that we discuss in the next chapter – one that is easy and affordable to implement, but also highly effective in getting you in front of your ideal prospects.

⌘ ⌘ ⌘

Direct Mail: The Easy Way to Spread Your Message Within Your Local Community

Direct Mail and Every Door Direct Mail (EDDM) in particular, is one of the most cost-effective ways to get in front of your local ideal customer. The majority of most local businesses customers come from within a five mile radius of the business location. Because of this EDDM is especially effective.

One example is when you've done a job in a certain neighborhood, you can leverage that job via an EDDM mailing, to get your customer's neighbors to also become your customers. Simply send an EDDM postcard that includes your customer's 5-star review of your work along with a special incentive for taking action now.

Most small businesses can't afford TV, radio, or billboard advertising, but Direct Mail is the least expensive, most effective way for a small business to blanket a neighborhood with your marketing message.

Whether you use a consumer list comprised of prospective customers who have recently reached a specific milestone – buying a home, for instance, or you use EDDM to mail to every address on a specific mail route, you'll want to have a solid strategy in place before you mail your first piece. Map out the entire sequence of mailings, calls to action, and follow-up actions that you'll use, and be sure to include tracking and metrics to ensure the best return on your marketing investment.

Ray L. Perry
www.RayLPerry.com
www.MarketBlazer.com
www.NeedMarketing.com

Receive a free copy of Ray's book *Renewable Referrals*.
Visit www.raylperry.com/business-marketing-audit
for details.

⌘ ⌘ ⌘

Chapter Eleven: Be the Host with the Most (Leads, that Is)

> *"We cannot live only for ourselves.*
> *A thousand fibers connect us with our fellow men."*

Herman Melville

Events are a form of content marketing, and if you're smart, you'll use them to broadcast your message, find leads, and convert those leads into customers.

Especially for a small business, though, this can prove challenging. Many people aren't clear on how, exactly, to host an event effectively. Even more confusing is how to sponsor or exhibit at someone else's event without simply wasting time and money, but to instead use it as a powerful lead-generation device.

The thing about events, though, is that they offer one very valuable benefit: a lot of face time. You get to stand in front of prospective customers, sharing your important message with them. They see your face, they see your brand, and they often see your business location itself. All of this helps build trust with your potential market, and encourages people to give your products or services a try.

A common mistake, however, is to throw an event or sign on to sponsor another organization's event, then dust off your hands and trust that customers will roll in. While some may, you will not get nearly as much interest as you would with a targeted plan that makes use of the community around you, the connections you can build in the process and the specific contributions you have to offer to prospective customers or clients. That's what we're going to cover right now.

Event and Sponsorship 101

First things first. While you might think you know the definitions of event and sponsorship, the shape they take for the purpose of small business marketing may not be that familiar to you, and that's okay. Let's take a look at each.

An event can take many forms, but broadly speaking, it is a special occasion hosted by your business to which various people are invited. Depending on your goals and your business, you may invite only a select audience of high-powered prospects, or you might open your arms to an entire neighborhood. An event's main benefit is that it puts you in front of a large crowd and allows you to broadcast your message.

What kinds of events can you do?

- Educational workshops (hosted by you or in conjunction with others)
- Trade Shows (typically produced by another organization)
- Seminars
- Holiday-themed parties
- Open houses
- Customer appreciation events
- and many, many more

If you don't have the money, time or energy to host your own events, you can try sponsorships. When you sponsor an event, you are in a sense riding the coattails of the person hosting it… and if you plan carefully you can get many of the same benefits as hosting your own event without all the work that entails.

For example, imagine there was an organization in your community who was having a well-known speaker visit for an event they were hosting. They needed sponsors to help pay the speaker's fee, and as part of the sponsorship they were offering a few minutes on stage at the event to speak about your business. They would also provide sponsors with the full list of attendees so that you could follow up with them. This would be a great opportunity for you to get some face time with potential customers… but ONLY if the speaker in question was aligned to your type of business, and would attract your target audience. For example, Dave Ramsey, the notable money management speaker, would be a perfect choice for:

- Life insurance companies
- Banks
- Financial planners
- Tax professionals
- Accountants
- Divorce lawyers
- and others who deal with finances and money management in any capacity

You can also attend events such as trade shows, where you have a huge chance of interacting with potential customers. This is essentially a form of sponsoring, since you're paying for a vendor booth where you will have the opportunity to introduce your business to attendees but you haven't done most of the work in setting up or paying for the event.

Advertising Sponsorships Versus Community Goodwill Sponsorships

Let's take a second and detour to discuss the difference between advertising sponsorships and community goodwill sponsorships. Helping the community for nothing in return is an excellent way to raise awareness for a cause and give back to the community that you care about. Sponsoring a 10K race that raises money for local charities and getting your logo on the back of the race T-shirt in return is a perfect example of a community goodwill sponsorship.

It is not, however, the same as an advertising sponsorship, which has the specific goal of gaining new customers for your business. In the above example, a person running in the race would not be likely to change accountants just because they saw the logo for Smith and Co. Accounting on the back of a T-shirt. However, if a local athletic shoe store was sponsoring the race, and as part of their sponsorship got the names and emails of everyone who registered for the race so that they could send them information about their upcoming shoe sale or selling admissions to a new group training program, that would be an advertising sponsorship. The difference between the two is the likelihood of the business actually getting new customers from the sponsorship.

Because you must pay for sponsorships, if your intent is to acquire new customers for your business as a part of the sponsorship, make sure before you make the investment that you have a great plan in mind for how that sponsorship is going to generate leads and grow your business. What is the plan? What will people do in response? How will that grow your business?

If you are simply supporting a cause, of course, the lead generation plan isn't important. Just don't confuse a cause with an advertising sponsorship and then be surprised when it doesn't engender results. Since you are not targeting your niche market nearly as carefully as you would be with an advertising sponsorship, it probably won't result in new business, but that's ok. This is a good argument for not funding community goodwill sponsorships out of the marketing budget; it really isn't marketing.

Of course, creating relationships with bigger organizations that can help you – such as the Chamber of Commerce, for instance – can be an important move, even if that relationship doesn't directly result in new business right away. For example, sponsoring a table at the annual Chamber awards banquet probably won't result directly in new customers, but it might help build up some goodwill with the Chamber that can be cashed in down the road when you need help. Otherwise, though, make sure you're receiving something of value from the sponsorship: getting to attend the event, make physical contacts with potential customers, pulling traffic through your own door.

You can improve your ability to target the right sponsorship opportunities by asking and answering these two questions:

- How will I capture leads?
- How will I follow up with them once I do?

Before you sponsor an event, ensure that you will get time in front of the audience to talk to them and broadcast your message. Think of this as making a special offer, one that at least some of them won't be able to refuse.

How Do You Use Events to Generate Leads?

When you throw an event or sponsor someone else's, your plan is important and needs to be thought through. You can't show up with a big bowl of candy and hope that's going to do the job; you've got to put in the time and energy to get it right. Whether you host or sponsor an event, you have to use it to get in front of customers, and then you need to be sure you have something to say that they will respond to. Your call to action must be clear, easy to understand and concise, and it must involve a time element, a reason to do it now.

Trade Shows – Use "Give to Get"

At a trade show, for instance, it isn't enough to simply set out a pile of brochures and hope people will take one. If you do this, you're most likely wasting the money you paid to attend the event (and the money you spent on printing brochures). Instead, you can use any of the following techniques, or more than one:

- A signup sheet where people can join your email list
- A sweepstakes that people can enter to win a prize after providing contact information
- A free consultation with you, as long as they schedule it on the spot
- A free ticket to your next workshop in exchange for their name and email address
- A free book, DVD, or other education content in exchange for their name and phone number

Do you see a pattern here? All of the above methods allow you to control the follow up process by capturing the contact information of the people you interact with. Never hand a brochure to someone who seems interested in your business and let them walk away from your booth without asking for their contact information. There's an excellent chance that you'll never hear from them again, and that your brochure will end up in the trashcan outside the event venue.

Host Your Own Workshop

At a workshop, people have paid to attend and learn from you or your host. Once the workshop is over, you must have a clear next step for people to take, and that next step must be clearly linked to what they just learned. If it isn't, your message will be disjointed and people won't take the bait. So for example, a print shop might sponsor a marketing materials seminar, offering attendees a discount on their first order.

Another good example of a way to capture leads at a workshop is a feedback form, on which a host asks for suggestions for making the workshop better, things attendees would like to see, a synopsis of what they learned, and so on. At the top, you as the host can offer a selection of downloadable goods they can get from your website. All they have to do is give you their email so you can send them a link to access the material. It moves value in both directions, isn't sleazy, and gives you another opportunity to prove your worth to them. It also is a value-add to the host for them to show all the "extras" event attendees get for coming.

Or you can offer a copy of your book in exchange for a one-on-one consultation. Especially if you are in a business where a one-on-one practically guarantees conversion, then this move will be totally worthwhile. Whether its your own event or someone else's, giving something away for free in exchange for moving a potential customer down your sales funnel is a great move.

No matter what you do, always make sure that the lead generation technique you use matches your goal for the event. If you want to grow your email list, encourage people to give you or trade you for an email. If you want more business, offer consultations that get you in front of people one-on-one, and so on.

How to Use Your Sponsorships Wisely

Many people understand how to apply the above lessons to an event, but are confused when it comes to sponsoring. Unfortunately, it's not enough to smack your logo on someone else's promotional materials, throw out a stack of brochures and call it good. If you are actually spending the money to sponsor someone else's event, it should get you attention, leads and prospective customers who want to take the next step… which means you must also know what that next step is.

Yet a surprising number of people sponsor events, then don't bother to pass out flyers or brochures, interact with the attendees on a personal level, or take advantage of the small segments of time allotted to them to do a commercial spot. This makes no sense, and only wastes the time and energy you invested in reaching out, connecting and making the sponsorship happen.

So how can you get more from your sponsorships? Start by taking advantage of every marketing opportunity offered to you. If you have a speaking slot, use the full amount of time to describe your business and what you offer customers. When allowed, take the time to pass out materials to attendees. Shake hands, make personal connections, and don't be shy. You needn't feel as if you're stealing the spotlight simply by taking your hosts up on their end of the bargain. If there is a strict prohibition on self-promotion during your talk, then structure your talk as a case study centered on solving a problem common in your business that many in the audience would have experienced. Doing this positions you as an expert without sounding like you've done a "hard sell" on your products and services. You do not even have to mention your company by name, it will be assumed that you are describing a challenge you are an expert in addressing.

When you present your special offer, make sure it is actually appealing to the prospect. If you sell expensive products or services, a 10% discount may not get them in the door. A higher one, on the other hand, might. Or you could hold a sweepstakes where you give away a product or service to one person for free. This is usually pretty budget-friendly, because it's only one item in exchange for a whole bunch of leads. Plus, you automatically know that the people who sign up are interested in what you offer, so you can begin marketing to them.

Lastly, take any opportunity you can to follow up. If the host gives you a list of attendees who have granted permission to be contacted, by all means use it.

Leveraging Your Event Beyond the Event

Really smart businesses don't let the event die with the closing bell; they repurpose the content over and over again. One of the easiest ways to do this, whether you host an event of your own or give a presentation at another organization's event, is to record the material. You can then turn it into:

- Segmented videos to use on your website
- Smaller segments to bulk up your YouTube channel
- Clips to use on your social media platforms

- Transcripts that become blog posts, email marketing materials or informational products
- Audio downloads

This not only provides you with excellent content you don't have to create anew, it furnishes you with social credibility. People who watch those clips or videos or listen to those transcripts in future are receiving proof that others consider you an expert. Most people are more willing to give their time, money and trust to you when they see that lots of others have already done the same.

Also, when you participate in an event someone else is hosting, promote the event through your own channels (website, social media, email, etc.) as a way to draw your customers and prospects to the event. This not only helps you with your target customers but also tells the host that you're the kind of participant they want back in the future as you help make the overall event successful.

That's All Folks!

Well, not really. You'll need to make serious effort to integrate these lessons into your marketing plan, but done right, events and sponsorships can be an excellent way to build your business. Just remember that you can be a fabulous form of content marketing for your brand, and that the way you approach events and sponsorships can either make smart use of your time and money, or waste it.

The steps listed in this chapter will help you take the smart approach, every time. We're barreling down on the end of this book now that we've discussed live events and sponsorships, but what's coming next may be the most useful section yet. Are you ready to get an action plan you can use to implement what you've learned?

⌘ ⌘ ⌘

Case Study: Insurance Agent Hosts and Grows

David Wise is an independent insurance agent specializing in agribusiness (www.DavidWise.com). One of the tactics he uses to generate leads is putting on free workshops for the Virginia Cooperative Extension, an educational outreach program of Virginia's land-grant universities. He hosts the workshops together with a strategic partner of his, an attorney who specializes in estate planning and small business law. Workshop topics include how to set up the appropriate legal entity for a business, planning for long-term medical care, and estate planning. David shares the costs of promoting the workshop with his partner, and they both invite their current clients and any guests their clients want to bring (as well as the general public). Over the years, the workshops have been a great source of new clients for both David and his strategic partner. He even had a video recording of a workshop made and posted online so that those who weren't able to attend could still watch it.

Kevin Jordan
www.redpointmarketingconsultants.com

⌘ ⌘ ⌘

Chapter Twelve: Getting Started

"Things may come to those who wait, but only the things left by those who hustle."

Abraham Lincoln

Congratulations! If you're reading this right now, it means you've made it almost all the way to the end of our book, and that means you're the kind of person who finishes what you start and follows through on your commitments. The fact that you're even reading a book like this to begin with indicates that you've made a commitment to grow your business and improve your marketing, so right now you're probably itching to start implementing some of the tactics you've learned in the book. We'd like to wrap it all up by suggesting a plan of attack to help you get started.

Strategy First

For most of this book, we've been discussing various marketing tactics you can use to generate leads, from direct mail to online marketing. Depending on how fast a reader you are, days, weeks, or even months may have passed since you first started reading the book (hey, we know how busy things can get as a small business owner—we won't judge). However, if it has been a while since you read Chapter Two (about creating a marketing strategy for your business), we suggest that you begin by re-reading that chapter.

We know, we know... marketing strategy isn't the most exciting or sexy subject on the planet. It's not nearly as exciting as all the fun marketing tactics we discuss throughout the book. You know what else isn't fun or exciting? Spending hundreds or thousands of dollars on a marketing tactic that fails to generate a single lead for your business because there was no strategy behind it. As small business marketing consultants who have decades of experience working with local business owners, we see this problem all the time.

The fact is that any type of marketing campaign, no matter how well executed, will not be very successful if it is not narrowly targeted at a well-defined ideal customer, and does not communicate well the unique selling proposition of the business in question. In chapter two we suggest several specific exercises that will help you identify your ideal customer and unique selling proposition. Complete these exercises before jumping in to marketing tactics, or risk wasting your time and money.

Content Next

Once you have a marketing strategy in place, spend some time creating or updating educational content that supports your core message. Remember the marketing kit from Chapter Three? Spend some time creating one for your business, and then re-purpose the content you create for that in as many different ways as you can to save time. Like plotting your strategy, this is another step you may be tempted to skip—do so at your own risk. In addition to lack of marketing strategy, lack of good educational content is another top reason for the failure of many marketing campaigns.

Create Your Online Presence

After you have created your foundational content, it's time to put that content online so people can find it. We strongly recommend hiring a professional to help you design a high-quality website and optimize it for online search. The particulars change so quickly in the world of online marketing that it's just too difficult for you, the busy small business owner, to keep abreast of what the current "best practices" are. Even in the six months that it took us to create this book, there have been several significant developments in this area that caused us to go back and revise sections we had previously written. If you're reading this book more than six months after it was published, some of what we've said about websites and SEO may have changed—that's just the nature of the beast. Let someone who knows what they're doing help you establish your online presence so that you can focus on what you do best—running your business.

After you have your core website set up, move on to other areas of your online presence like directory listings, social media platforms, and ratings and review sites. Create a plan for maintaining and monitoring your online presence so that you don't end up with the "ghost town" effect we describe in Chapter Eight.

Work on ONE tactic at a time

When you're ready to start trying some of the various marketing tactics we discuss in the book, we strongly recommend that you focus on implementing one marketing tactic at a time, perfecting that tactic, and creating a system for maintaining your progress and results before moving on to the next tactic. For example, let's say that you aren't currently doing any email marketing, and after reading Chapter Eight you decide that's something you really need to try. You might use the following action plan to tackle this:

1. Create a professional email address using your domain, if you don't already have one.
2. Research various email marketing services and decide which one is best for your needs.
3. Add a sign-up form for your email list to your website and come up with a compelling reason for people to fill it out.
4. Create a template for your email newsletter and decide how often you're going to send it.
5. Set up an auto-responder series of emails that people will get after first joining your email list.
6. Send your first few email newsletters, track your open and click-thru rates, and compare them to industry standards.
7. Decide who will be responsible for writing and sending your email newsletter going forward, and delegate that task to them (either someone on your staff, or someone you are outsourcing this to).

If you devote an hour or two a week to the tasks listed above, you can easily accomplish them all within a month, and then you can move on to focus on another tactic the next month while continuing to build your email list.

However, if you immediately go out and try to implement all the tactics we suggest in this book, you probably won't do any of them very well, and will likely get overwhelmed and discouraged very quickly. Pick the two or three tactics you think would give you the best return on investment (in terms of both time and money), focus on implementing one at a time, and after a few months of persistent effort you'll have them all nailed.

Put it on the calendar
Notice we said that after a few months of persistent effort you would have them all nailed. That's different than two weeks of persistent effort, followed by three weeks of no progress while you deal with a mini-crisis that has popped up in your business, followed by two weeks of half-hearted attempts to get back on track... you know the drill. Pick a day of the week and schedule at least an hour on that day at the same time every week to work on your marketing. If other staff members need to be involved in the process, make sure they block the time off as well so that you can meet to discuss your progress. Don't cancel these meetings at the drop of a hat whenever anything else needs your attention—give them the same level of priority as you would your best client.

Get Help If You Need It

All the authors of this book are small business owners, and we fully realize how difficult it can be to manage all aspects of your business while trying to implement new ideas—especially when implementing those ideas may require technical expertise that you or your staff don't have. If you need assistance with any of the marketing tactics we describe in this book, we are ready and willing to help you. We work with local business owners just like you every day who are probably struggling with the same issues you are when it comes to your marketing. We use proven processes and systems to help them overcome their problems, and we'd like to use those systems to help you as well.

There is nothing more frustrating for us than to watch a small business implement a poorly planned and executed marketing campaign that was doomed from the start, all the while knowing exactly what could have been done differently to make it successful. It's even more painful when we know the business in question has a limited marketing budget, and probably couldn't really afford not to get results from whatever tactic they were attempting. The last thing we'd want is for this to happen to you. If you need help or have any questions at all, please don't be afraid to reach out to us. We all do free consultations, and would be happy to give you some pointers to help you get started on the right track, even if you don't end up hiring us to assist you.

The moment of truth

Now that you've reached the end of the book, it's time to take action. Before you put this book down, take out a pen and paper and write down three specific tasks you will complete within the next seven days to begin implementing what you have learned in your business. Then, get out your calendar (still before putting the book down, mind you), and schedule time to work on those tasks.

Ok, now you can put the book down…but keep it close at hand as a reference as you begin working on your tasks. You'll also want to visit our website for additional resources related to the content of each chapter of the book:

www.LocalLeadGenBook.com/resources

In addition, if you purchased this book yourself instead of "borrowing" it from a friend, you can access the following bonuses on our website by providing proof of purchase:

- A bonus chapter about video marketing
- Free copy of the book Renewable Referrals (100 copies available on a first come, first serve basis)

- A free eBook entitled 66 Local Lead Generation Tactics by the authors of this book, listing some of the most effective tactics we've used with our clients
- Free copies of six eBooks published by Duct Tape Marketing, including Seven Steps to Small Business Marketing Success—which describes how to create a complete marketing system for your business
- Video interviews with all of the authors, in which we each discuss our areas of expertise in more detail
- An infographic created by one of the authors detailing exactly how to lay out a website for a local business for optimal SEO and lead conversion results
- A step-by-step, fill-in-the-blank template you can use to create a marketing kit for your business, as described in chapter three

Visit www.LocalLeadGenBook.com/special-offers to grab those bonuses.

That's all the content we've got for you – now get out there and start generating those leads!

About the Authors

Mark Z. Fortune
Fortune Marketing, LLC
www.fortunemarketinginc.com

Mark Z. Fortune is the founder of Fortune Marketing, LLC, a marketing consultancy for small businesses based in Little Rock, Arkansas. Building on a 20-year career in sales and marketing for companies ranging from the Fortune 100 to start ups, Mark opened Fortune Marketing to provide small business owners with a simple, practical, and effective system for growth. As a Certified Duct Tape Marketing Consultant Mark installs marketing systems that help small business owners sleep better at night knowing they have a plan and system for attracting and retaining customers.

Mark works with clients as a coach, advisor, or as a marketing strategy and implementation partner to ensure sales and marketing investments return positive results. He believes the most exciting part of the marketing world is working with small businesses because:

- Sales and marketing challenges are not insurmountable and can be met with a disciplined and focused approach to sales and marketing leveraging the principles of the Duct Tape Marketing System
- The technology and media landscape today makes it easier than ever before for a small business to compete and win against large competitors
- Small businesses are fun to work with, and results are easiest to see in small businesses; if something doesn't work, it's easiest to change in a small business
- Life is too short to spend the majority of your time doing things that aren't fun, aren't productive or aren't leading to positive results.

Mark's marketing and sales experience includes teaching at the university level, running a global sales support and marketing organization, launching the first text messaging products for a wireless carrier and promoting bands to independent music stores (back when such stores still existed).

Follow Mark Z Fortune:
Twitter: @FortuneMktgInc
Facebook: facebook.com/fortunemktginc
LinkedIn: www.linkedin.com/in/markzfortune

Kevin Jordan

Redpoint Marketing Consultants

RedpointMarketingConsultants.com

Kevin is the owner of Redpoint Marketing Consultants and the host of the Small Business Marketing Minute show, a video and audio podcast that teaches simple, affordable, and practical marketing methods to small business owners.

Prior to starting his consulting business, Kevin spent six years as an airline pilot for US Airways Express before leaving that career to become an entrepreneur.

Thanks to his training as a pilot, Kevin has a unique understanding of how well-run systems can dramatically improve efficiency. Using that philosophy, Kevin focuses on helping local, service-based businesses create complete marketing systems, and then runs those systems for them on an ongoing basis.

Kevin is also a public speaker and regularly teaches workshops on small business marketing for local chambers of commerce and other organizations that support small businesses. Workshop topics include email marketing, video marketing, website best practices, and of course the Duct Tape Marketing system. He's been a member of the Duct Tape Marketing Consultant Network since 2012.

Kevin is a native of Indiana and graduate of Purdue University, and currently resides in Virginia with his wife Jen. In his spare time he enjoys backpacking, rock climbing, home brewing, and fishing.

Follow Kevin Jordan:
Twitter: @RMCVirginia
Facebook: facebook.com/RedpointMarketingConsultants
LinkedIn: linkedin.com/in/kevinjordan247

Ray L. Perry
MarketBlazer, Inc.
www.RayLPerry.com
www.MarketBlazer.com
www.NeedMarketing.com

Ray is a Marketing Consultant, Business Advisor, Author of "Guide to Marketing your Business Online" (2011), "Renewable Referrals" (2014), "The Small Business Owners Guide to Local Lead Generation" (2015) and a Certified Duct Tape Marketing Consultant.

As a Certified Duct Tape Marketing Consultant Ray helps his clients develop marketing strategies to find prospects that have a need for their products and services, and engage those prospects to know, like, and trust his clients, becoming long-term customers. This can further result in these new customers referring his clients' to other potential customers with the same need or problem.

Ray is the Chief Marketing Officer with MarketBlazer, Inc., a technology based marketing agency specializing in lead generation and lead conversion. As a marketing company focused on helping small businesses grow, they combine a proven marketing process and strong technology background with the latest in internet, social media and mobile marketing tactics to develop solid long-term marketing strategies for their clients. Their goal with marketing is simple and straightforward: To help every client's business thrive!

Follow Ray L. Perry:
www.linkedin.com/in/raylperry
www.plus.google.com/+rayperry
www.twitter/raylperry

Phil Singleton
Kansas City Web Design®
www.KCWebDesigner.com

Phil Singleton is founder of The Kansas City Marketing Agency™, a small business marketing consulting agency based in Kansas City, MO, and a Duct Tape Marketing Certified Consultant. Phil has a B.S. In Finance from Fairfield University and an MBA from Thunderbird, The Graduate School of International Management in Phoenix, Arizona. Phil is also the author of the book New SEO: Search Engine Optimization For Web Designers & Business Owners.

A finance guy by training, Phil is laser-focused on ROI which explains why he is passionate about helping companies generate more phone call leads, email inquiries and referrals. Small business marketing consulting, with a focus on web design and SEO, is just a means to this end. Phil believes that the Internet drives more purchase decisions than any other medium in the history of capitalism, and as such has devoted the last ten years working with companies of all sizes to dominate search engine rankings. In addition to providing small business marketing consulting services to companies in the Midwest, Phil provides SEO-friendly custom websites under the brand Kansas City Web Design® and online marketing and search engine optimization services under the brand Kansas City SEO®.

Phil is an active blogger and his content and blog posts have been featured on Duct Tape Marketing, Freshbooks, SEMRush, Ahrefs.com, Advanced Web Ranking, WebDesignerDepot.com, Business2Community.com and many local Kansas City area and Midwest regional print publications and websites.

Some unique highlights of Phil's Career include:

- Helped dozens of US startups and tech companies raise strategic venture capital investment (over $20 million) and cross-border licensing agreements in the Asia Pacific region.
- Ran the global retail and online sales divisions for a best-selling line of consumer software products
- Started a software company in Asia, raising over $1M in venture capital funding, grew to profitability with 25 employees, then sold three years later. This experience in what got him into SEO and Internet marketing…in short by following the ROI trail to SEO.
- Is fluent in Mandarin Chinese
- Lived in Asia for over 10 years, primarily in Taipei, Taiwan, and briefly in Beijing, Shanghai & Hong Kong.
- Lives in Overland Park, KS with wife Vivian and twin sons Ely & Ostyn

Follow Phil Singleton:
https://twitter.com/kcwebsites
https://plus.google.com/+PhilSingleton
https://www.linkedin.com/in/seokansascity

Justin Sturges

Systemadik

www.Systemadik.com

Justin has been working online since 1994 and in local SEO, website building and lead generation for over a decade. His efforts sell millions of dollars worth of products and services for his local clients each year. His systems help business rank, get more traffic, convert more sales, generate more leads and tell a unique and compelling story online.

Ranking and being found are not enough anymore though. Now, you have to stand out, have an amazing website and tell a unique story that your ideal prospects appreciate.

Very few marketing shops in the local space provide the comprehensive support and expertise it requires to succeed online across channels. Justin's team at Systemadik manage comprehensive systems including; websites, local SEO, social media, blog creation and content, advertising on Google and Facebook, email marketing, design, and various lead generation channels.

One of Justin's claims to local marketing fame is being the author of the infographic "The Local Small Business SEO Guide" which was featured on the Copyblogger Authority webinar series, the Duct Tape Marketing blog, and many others.

Based on this local SEO blueprint, Justin's team has created a platform for local business websites called the "Local Marketing System" or LMS. The system combines location optimization, landing pages, review tools, special offer management, mobile responsive capabilities, email tools and much more. There is not a more robust local website and marketing system available. Contact the Systemadik team for more information on how the system can help your local business.

Contact Justin Sturges:
www.systemadik.com
justin@systemadik.com

Made in the USA
Lexington, KY
30 January 2016